A Guide to Short-Term Missions

A Comprehensive Manual for
Planning an Effective Mission Trip

by

H. Leon Greene, M.D.

Gabriel
Publishing

Waynesboro, Georgia, U.S.A.

Published by Gabriel Publishing.
PO Box 1047, 129 Mobilization Dr
Waynesboro, GA 30830 U.S.A.
(706) 554-1594
gabriel@omlit.om.org

Library of Congress Cataloging-in-Publication Data available.

Cover design: Paul Lewis

CONTENTS

WHY WRITE A BOOK
ABOUT SHORT-TERM MISSIONS?

In the jungles of Honduras with Youth With A Mission (YWAM), I learned some of my first lessons about short-term missions. Our group leader, Andrew Wark, a delightful chap from Australia, told me a few secrets for a successful mission experience. First, the informal motto of YWAM was "At all times be ready to sing, pray, preach, or die." The commitment to serve takes you outside of your comfort zone. Second, he told me to be flexible. (I like the bumper sticker that says, "Want to give God a good laugh? Tell Him what *you* think tomorrow holds.") Finally, he never failed to remind me that God is in control.

This book is written to encourage anyone who is about to undertake a short-term mission trip or just considering such an endeavor. I recently took a two-month short-term mission trip to a small village named Balfate on the northern coast of Honduras. Balfate is located in an area where poverty is the norm and extreme heat rules. I served as the only physician for a small medical clinic at a site where a hospital to serve the poor in the region is being built by a Christian organization. The location was quite remote and isolated. My wife, Judy, and our younger son, Matthew, joined me after two weeks to help with the work.

There I kept a journal, which I sent back home by e-mail to family, friends, and supporters every time I went to the main town, which was about fifty miles away, and had access to a phone line. The experiences were real and generally typical of any short-term mission trip. The notes from this journal or extended letter are reproduced in this book as the first part of each chapter just as I wrote them daily (with only minor editorial changes for clarity). On days when I went to town and could send e-mails, a new chapter begins. At times you'll have to ignore the medical references. Many of the recipients of these e-mails were nurses and doctors.

By reliving my experiences with me, you may begin to understand the dynamics of a short-term mission experience and how to make your own short-term mission successful. A short-term mission is indeed an ordained calling that should not be taken lightly. The rewards of a short-term mission can be inestimable, but they are not automatically guaranteed.

1

*"God doesn't call us because we're equipped,
He equips us for the call"*

What Is a Short-term Mission, and Does God Use It?

May 27

Hi, everyone!

United Airlines has me firmly in their corporate grasp (not to mention seatbelt) as we wing our way to Denver and then New Orleans. This is the first leg of the trip to Balfate, Colon, Honduras, Central America. (You know you're traveling a long distance when your destination has four identifiers.) Tomorrow I grab TACA Airlines (or vice versa) for Honduras.

Judy, Matthew, and I are going to Honduras for two months. We will be working with the Cornerstone Foundation, which operates a clinic on the north coast and is building a hospital there. The only doc for about 30,000 people at the edge of a mountainous jungle will be gone for the summer, and I will be taking his place. The clinic in Honduras should be quite busy. I will be challenged by a lot of medicine I've never seen or even thought about. I just have to remember that if I weren't there, they'd have no medical care. So I just have to try to be better than nothing. Not as easy as it sounds.

Because there are no phones, faxes, mail, or e-mail available, we will be incommunicado. We will emerge in two months from the canopy of trees and the fellowship with the monkeys. We will be perplexed strangers to the world that no doubt has done quite well without us.

Many folks have asked that we keep them informed about our journey, so we will try to keep a diary (not a dairy, though that might be useful too) of our adventures. So this group e-mail will begin to relate our experiences and the answers to all of your prayers. Your first prayer—that I leave town soon—has already been answered.

Many of you are medically oriented, many of you are connected to us through church, some of you are family, and a few of you fall into many categories. For some, these notes will be too theological; for others, too clinical; and for most, too impersonal. What an opportunity! A chance to offend everyone! A few of you are recent acquaintances, and you might find all of my thoughts tedious. That's the beauty of e-mail. You're just a click away from the recycle bin. Use it as you see fit.

We always think that we will discover some exotic new disease on a trip like this or, even better, find its rare cure. Or that we will happen upon some new theological insight. But usually we just expend all of our energies on finding clean water, cooking rice, and rinsing the sweat off our collective brow. The mundane once again supplants the ethereal.

I am in what most mission agencies call the "first phase" of the trip. Maybe you are unfamiliar with the stages of a mission trip. If so, I'll identify them for you below.

Phase 1: That time during which you try to stay clean and dry and succeed. This phase usually lasts about five to ten minutes after arrival at the intended destination.

Phase 2: That time during which you try to stay clean and dry and fail. Your ultimate success is likely to depend upon how firmly you cling to this goal. If you keep this objective, you will become a very unhappy camper, questioning why God is punishing you or allowing your job to be thwarted.

Phase 3: That time during which you remain dirty and wet and don't care. This phase should last at least a few weeks or months. Your success on the trip is critically dependent upon your ability to accept the conditions where you are working without complaining or, more accurately, without really caring about the circumstances.

Phase 4: That time during which you think you are going to die and are afraid that you will. This phase is a sign that it is time to go home. With the grace of God, your project will be complete by the time this phase arrives, the next replacement will be arriving soon, and you will be able to hang on.

Phase 5: That time during which you think you are going to die and are afraid that you won't. Pray that you don't reach this phase.

While these descriptions may seem impious, they accurately reflect the stages we anticipate.

Time to go. The plane is about to land, and they're asking, "Is there a pilot on board?"

On the road to Honduras,
Leon Greene

———————————————

What is a short-term mission? Should we endorse it? Mission work is often defined by the length of service. Anything less than two years is a short-term mission. Sometimes distinctions are made among the various types of mission trips.

- Career mission: Longer than two years.
- Short-term mission: Less than two years with a clearly defined goal or project.
- Cultural exposure: Less than four weeks with broad goals or purposes, often multifaceted.
- Vacation with a purpose: Usually less than two weeks with limited goals, often being to support and encourage long-term missionaries. (Frequently these trips are made by a family, and some real vacation time is included.)

What are the advantages and disadvantages of these missions? A short-term mission has many advantages:

- It is a direct response to God's command to go into all nations.
- It teaches the practical application of the Great Commission.
- It causes you to grow in your Christian walk.
- It gives new and expanded vistas of the Christian experience.
- It raises the importance of missions for the home church.
- It gives insight into God's kingdom worldwide.
- It enriches and encourages career missionaries on the field.
- It inspires people to consider long-term service.
- It frees the career missionaries from some of their work load.
- You learn about your church's missionaries, their

needs, struggles, and victories.

- You learn firsthand about the need for prayer and how to pray for the missionaries.
- You learn about different cultures, many of which know nothing about Jesus.
- You learn about the needs of Christians in other lands.
- You become corresponding friends with missionaries.
- You experience the unity of the body of Christ worldwide.
- You learn how to share your faith—it can actually be easier to share it for the first time in a foreign setting.
- You become emotionally and spiritually tied to another church or congregation.
- You minister to the spiritually hungry; they minister to your hunger as well.
- You deliver much-needed equipment and supplies to the long-term missionaries.
- Short-term missions are almost guaranteed to have a long-term positive effect on the people who go— very few activities can make this claim at a cost that is justifiable.
- It contributes your specific skills to complete a project, such as the following:
    - Medical/dental care
    - Construction
    - Evangelism
    - Discipling
    - Teaching (English as a second language, for example)
    - Church planting
    - Relief work
    - Repairs
    - Gardening
    - Cleaning
    - Maintenance
    - Children's ministries

However, there are also some disadvantages to short-term missions:

- They can be burdensome for the long-term missionaries (more trouble than they're worth).
- "Short termers" can be culturally insensitive and make problems for the long-term missionaries long after the short-term team has gone home.
- Short-term workers can suffer considerable culture shock and reverse culture shock. (It can be as distressing to return home to U.S. culture as it is to go to a developing country.)
- Often the short termer has little to contribute, especially if the preparation has been deficient.
- Language barriers can add to the difficulty of the mission—it may be impossible to relate meaningfully to the people of the country visited.
- The short-term missionary may react negatively to the host culture.
- Short-term missions are costly of both time and money.
- Short-term service can manifest guilt associated with having so many material possessions.
- Short-term missionaries may concentrate more on the project than the people to whom they're ministering.

It is important to acknowledge that there are valid questions that are asked about the utility and appropriateness of short-term missions. Certainly the projects are costly, averaging about $1000–2000 per person. Could that money be better spent? Remember the woman who poured expensive perfume on Jesus before His crucifixion? Her display was unusual, but Jesus certainly did not condemn it.

While he was in Bethany, reclining at the table in the home of a man known as Simon the Leper, a woman came with an alabaster jar of very expensive perfume, made of pure nard. She broke the jar and poured the perfume on his head.

Some of those present were saying indignantly to one another, "Why this waste of perfume? It could have been sold for more than a year's wages and the money given to the poor." And they rebuked her harshly.

"Leave her alone," said Jesus. "Why are you bothering her? She has done a beautiful thing to me. The poor you will always have with you, and you can help them any time you want. But you will not always have me. She did what she could. She poured perfume on my body beforehand to prepare for my burial. I tell you the truth, wherever the gospel is preached throughout the world, what she has done will also be told, in memory of her" (Mark 14:3–9).

Short-term missions have been criticized for their expense. Since many missionaries are barely able to make ends meet with their meager support checks, shouldn't we just divert the short-term money to the full-time missionaries? My answer is that we do not have to make a choice. We can and should do both. Increasing the support of the full-time workers is necessary, but one way to accomplish this task is to educate specifically the younger members of the congregation about the missionaries' needs. Youth are most commonly engaged in the short-term mission effort. If you asked a more probing question, the answer might become obvious: "Would you spend $1000–2000 to alter indelibly the mindset of a young person, to establish a worldview of missions, to help a young person mature spiritually, to inspire fervent prayer for missionaries, to change a life, and perhaps to plant the seed of a future missionary?" Most people would answer yes to such a question.

Short-term missions are burgeoning. In 1979, 25,000 people participated in short-term missions. By 1989, the number had increased to 120,000. In 1995 it was up to 200,000,[1] and in 1999, over half a million people participated in short-term missions.[2] If you use that number to calculate mission investment at $1,000 per person, it becomes $500 million—quite a sizable chunk of money. We must be sure it is being used well. But for perspective, compare this money to the amount spent yearly worldwide on chewing gum, for example—over $2 billion. We in the United States alone spend over $6 billion yearly on video games and nearly $14 billion yearly on CDs and tapes. The expenditure on short-term missions, therefore, actually seems insufficient by comparison.

Is this short-term mission pattern just a fad? Has it simply become the rite of passage for youth involved in church activities? Is it necessary? Does the short-term mission trip merely represent a socially acceptable form of (often youthful) self-indulgence? To answer, we must examine whether the person going is responding to God's call and whether the short-term mission produces godly fruits in the host environment, in the person who goes on the trip, and in the sending congregation.

Most short-term mission workers have an entirely

positive approach. They accept the local conditions. They look for unique ways to serve. They are flexible. Most return home with a new or renewed sense of purpose to their lives, some with a vision that they didn't have before. Most are changed people, and that change can last a lifetime. They look at the world in a different way. They begin to understand the Great Commission. It becomes relevant in their local community of "Jerusalem" as well as in Judea, Samaria, and in the uttermost parts of the earth.

Through many years of doing short-term missions, I've seen countless youth who dedicate their lives to full-time Christian service as a result of their experiences in a foreign land. Pastors are born, missionaries are molded, and health-care workers—doctors, nurses, and physician's assistants—are inspired. Yes, I've also seen adults changed in ways that no other experience could have accomplished.

One of our children's leaders in our church has been a committed, evangelistic Christian for many years. She had devoted her life to the Christian cause, so she was no slouch as far as dedication is measured. But she had never been out of the country to see the church in the rest of the world. Recently she had the opportunity to go to Manila for two weeks as a children's educational worker. She felt "a personal awakening to the needs of the world's children," a concept she only thought she understood before the trip.

Listen to what she said to our church's missions committee: "Now I have a taste of desperation that children, who are some of the richest soil in which to plant the Truth, are not included in the plans as churches are planted all over the world." She saw children "warehoused" in a newly planted church while the adults learned to worship. They were "corralled into a small room with little or no direction, teaching, or learning for two long hours. What a waste of spiritually rich time and potential." This dear saint returned to the United States a changed woman! The first time we saw each other in church the next Sunday, she walked up to me and said simply, "Leon, now I understand!"

On the other hand, I've seen youth and adults alike who clearly should not have been members of a team. They spend the time feeling uncomfortable, complaining, and they don't develop a sense of mission. They want to go home from the moment they land in Unusualville. We cannot ignore the issues surrounding the preparation for the short-term ministry, such as the need to understand the culture, at least some of the language, and the effects of a team on the host missionary and culture.

Short-term missions can create monsters in the recipient culture as well. The medical work I did in Honduras last summer was rewarding in every way, and I could see God working in the hearts of the patients who came for treatment. Almost never did I experience any negative reactions from the Hondurans. Almost. We treated the poorest of the poor at our clinic. Virtually none of them had the means to travel to the "big city" for medical care. Many walked for hours in the hundred-degree heat to be seen in the clinic. Minor ailments were uncommon because it required so much determination just to get to the clinic. People only made the effort if they were seriously ill. Then the patients usually had to wait for hours to be seen.

But one day I saw a woman and her child in the mid-afternoon who looked strangely out of place. She was dressed quite well, and she even had a small gold necklace around her neck. She spoke some English, but we conversed in Spanish. She had only vague symptoms, nothing serious, though she persisted in describing them to me. When it came time for me to question and examine her child, I found few symptoms and signs. I then learned that they had come from a nearby town, driving a pickup through three rivers to reach us in Balfate. It would have been easier for them to go to the "big city" of La Ceiba than to come to our little clinic. I couldn't understand why she had come this direction, let alone why she had come at all since neither she nor her child were sick. As I finally insisted that it was time for me to see the next patient, she hesitatingly asked me in Spanish, *"Un dije?"* (A toy?) She had come to the clinic to get a toy for her daughter! Fearing that I did not understand her question, she repeated it in English, "A toy for my daughter?" She was quite offended when I told her that we did not have any toys for the children.

Previous medical teams to the area had brought toys to give to the children, and she expected that if her child came to the clinic held by this gringo she would get another toy. She did not know that I was here for two months and that we did not have a "brigade," a term used for large teams from the states that come for a week or two, often bringing many unneeded gifts for the Hondurans. She had learned to expect that outside help of any kind meant that people would be giving gifts. And strange enough, while this woman was the only person to ask for gifts, she was the richest person I saw for the entire two months that I worked in the clinic. Richness had produced greed (and perhaps vice versa also). But the image never left me.

A U.S. team can come and lavish goods upon the people causing them to miss the real reason for the team being there. We go to minister in God's name, but our own excesses can mask the message. We must be sure that our actions are well planned and that we do not send the wrong messages to the people to whom we are ministering. We are there to demonstrate God's love, not just to give them material things. I've also been to places where I've questioned whether decisions for Christ were sincere. Did the locals respond just because they knew that is what we wanted? How often had these same people "accepted Christ" when other teams were there? Serious food for thought.

What makes a good mission team? In simple numbers, a group of five to fifteen people seems to be a manageable size. A larger group can be difficult to house and feed. And transportation locally can be difficult. A smaller group may lack the critical mass to have the manpower and collective skills to accomplish a task. However, even a team of a few very skilled workers will always be valuable. Electricians, plumbers, nurses, worship leaders, teachers, and especially pastors are always needed. All must have willing hearts and go with an attitude of servitude and ambassadorship. They must be dedicated disciples, healthy in body and mature both in the faith and in demeanor. All team members must be well prepared, behave responsibly, and have the goals of winning souls, discipling lives, relieving distress, and working for the kingdom.

What are the logistics of a short-term mission trip? Arriving at your destination usually takes multiple forms of travel; rarely is only air transport sufficient. The team must be prepared to endure harsh conditions. The food will be simple. Clean water will be a luxury, and hot water will likely be only a dream. Electricity may be intermittent at best. Put simply, your team must be ready for a backwoods camping experience. The team should expect to pay the host for food, lodging, and local transportation, as primitive as these items may seem. Furthermore, the team must provide all materials for the work project or purchase them locally.

Missions teams can also be a drain on, rather than a blessing to, the missionaries. "A veteran Christian teacher in Beijing has had enough of short-term visitors from her home country. 'I used to think I could give them a briefing and orientation that could be helpful,' she told a mission agency leader. 'Very few ever listened. They all have their own agenda. All they want is instant results.' The woman now refuses to meet with such people and does not consider them to really be ministering to China."[3] Furthermore, short-term missionaries by definition can't personally see the long haul, nor do they adequately connect with the long-term workers. "'Short-term missionaries do not really get to know us,' an African believer told missionary Jim Lo. 'We may love them as brothers and sisters, but they are still strangers to us. It is hard to be influenced by strangers. We need more long-term missionaries than short-term missionaries.'"[4]

Tom Steller, missions pastor of Bethlehem Baptist Church in Minneapolis doesn't subscribe to the limited-pie theory of short-term missions. He is all for the boom. "'This is thrilling to me,' he said. 'I think it is a stimulation to missions. I don't think it is robbing missions dollars from long-term missionaries but rather widening the pool of informed missions supporters, both the returning short termers as well as the support networks they have tapped into.'"[5]

So we must be careful how we approach short-term missions. Stan Guthrie's statement summarizes short-term missions: "Short-term work, whether two weeks or two years, can indeed be effective and pleasing to God. Yes, it can cost a lot of money, disrupt nationals and missionaries, encourage short-term thinking, and inoculate some against career missions involvement. But done well, it can open participants' eyes to the some-times gritty realities of the world, make them aware of their own ethno-centrism and the gifts and courage of non-Western believers, and spark a lifelong commitment to missions. In the best cases, some real kingdom work gets done, too."[6]

2

"But I'm just a hairdresser!"

ARE YOU GIFTED FOR THE MISSION FIELD?

May 28 and 29
Greetings from Balfate!

As I was reading this morning in Ephesians 1, I was struck by the difference between the greetings of letters then and now. Were I living two thousand years ago, I might have begun by saying, "To all the saints in Woodinville, Bothell, and Seattle, the faithful in Christ Jesus. Grace and peace to you from God our Father and the Lord Jesus Christ."

The trip from New Orleans to Balfate was wondrously uneventful. Two flights were cancelled, and I still don't have my luggage, but the diversions were peaceful, even welcomed. I wound up taking a flight that deposited us on Roatan, the island off the north coast of Honduras where resorts are emerging and the scuba diving is rumored to be legendary. We were not allowed to leave the airplane, but the beauty of the reefs from the air beckons for a vacation trip someday.

I was met at the La Ceiba airport by Dave and Becky Drozek, the missionaries who are returning to *the States for the summer. They were still waiting at the gate even though my original flight was far past the cancellation stage. I had met another medical group on the flight since I had lots of time to visit while waiting for the next plane to La Ceiba. Their host was not at the airport, so we drove them (also without their luggage) to where they will be staying for the night*

Into action on the first day in Honduras. We saw about thirty-four patients in the clinic. A four-year-old girl was our first patient—severe asthma, quite weak, debilitated, lethargic to the point of somnolence. After her first two hours of treatment, she still looked bad, and we wondered if we might have to take her to town (through the rivers). After a different type of treatment (with medicine only slightly out of date) and some antibiotics and steroids, she recovered enough to go home by the day's end. But we will see her again tomorrow because she had bilateral pneumonia as well. Yes, a clinical diagnosis but one of certainty.

The clinic now is a wondrous creation. Patient flow approaches the precision of the legendary Swiss watch. The staff is motivated, dedicated, and even willing to tolerate gringos like me.

By the way, the rivers are down. On the trip to Balfate yesterday, the deepest spot was only about two feet, and the vehicle didn't even hesitate.

Prayer requests:

That my Spanish improve.

That I not gain any more weight (food is great).

That my Spanish improve quickly.

And, by the way, did I mention that my Spanish needs improving?

May 30
Last night I was reflecting on a person with diabetes whom we had seen in clinic yesterday. She had known about her diabetes for about one year. I asked Dr. Drozek how the diagnosis could have been made before he arrived. It turns out that the local Honduran Centro de Salud (healthcare center) is adept at improvising when equipment and supplies are lacking. They put a patient's urine in a small bowl on the ground. If the ants are drawn to it, then they assume there is sugar in the urine, and the person is given a diagnosis of diabetes. I asked how they monitor treatment. He said that when (and if) they have diabetes medication, they keep increasing the dose until the ants are no longer drawn to the urine. (Thanks, Bob, for the new medical lab kit, which we will use to improve on the urine-ant technique.)

Today we waded through the equipment that has been donated to the hospital. Unfortunately, most of it is beyond repair. There are some items that were made in the early 1970s, and they were sent here already broken and useless. But the hospital construction itself is proceeding nicely.

Tonight we went to church, which is held Tuesday, Thursday, Saturday, and Sunday. It consisted of the two pastors and their families, the worship leader and his son, about ten to fifteen other people, and us. I had a hard time following the message because the pastor spoke very rapidly. I was able to speak (through an interpreter) and simply encourage them to remain faithful. They are growing in their knowledge of the Bible, and the pastor (who was the same one we heard there in October) was quite well prepared and organized (according to the folks who could follow his rapid-fire Spanish).

May 31

Today was a clinic day. Beautiful sunrise, with what sounded like hundreds of birds singing. However, when I counted, it was only four. One bird comes to my window at precisely 5:30 in the morning. It is the same bird song I remember from last April and October. I am no longer setting my alarm, as a bird singing is much more pleasant. Here the preferred system is to get up very early and do some work before the sun gets too hot for outside work. Most folks in the village are already working at 5:00 or 6:00 a.m. It was 85 degrees early yesterday morning, and today was warmer. A clear day means the afternoon will be well over 100 degrees.

We saw forty patients today, but we probably should not be counting. Let me tell you about a few: One man, I'll call him Juan, had some heart and blood pressure problems (for the medical folks, he also has an abdominal aortic aneurysm) and came to clinic. I asked him how his heart was doing. He said, "Mi corazon es limpio! Jesus es en mi corazon." ("My heart is clean! Jesus is in my heart.") Juan has the correct perspective.

One lady, who I'll call Maria, had a baby one month ago. At the end of the clinic (after it was supposed to be closed) she appeared, having walked eight hours down from the mountains. We could not turn her away. Turns out, she had a high fever and tonsillitis. No doubt the eight-hour walk back was even harder for her.

Another woman, Violeta, is seventy-four years old. She had hypertension, cataracts, and aortic regurgitation. We performed what is probably the first electrocardiogram ever done in the state of Colon, certainly at least in the district (county) of Balfate. (For the medical folks, she had only LVH.)

Now (6:00 p.m.) it is raining torrentially. It probably won't last long. It is the dry season. Dr. Drozek and his family leave tomorrow, so we're hoping the rivers don't rise too much.

Thanks for all of your support. You are all in my prayers. My next e-mail will be June 14 at the earliest. That's the day that Judy and Matthew fly in to La Ceiba and will probably be the next day I'm coming to town.

(Okay guys, I know that a paragraph or two is fine to read, but multiply that amount of drivel by twelve days, and it becomes almost unbearable. So I won't be insulted if you only skim this letter.)

P.S. My luggage arrived intact!

Ever have questions about what God has in store for you? Do you wonder if God has a plan for your life? Have you ever questioned whether God could use you on the mission field? Are you valuable? Should you go on a short-term mission trip? We have all probably asked one or more of these questions at sometime in our lives, most of us in the last week or two.

My wife frequently ponders if she is really doing what God wants with her life. She thinks that she needs a title, a job description, or a new diploma (a bachelor of arts in English from Goucher College and a master of arts in teaching from George Washington University don't seem to count). About once each year, over the course of one or two months, she raises the question, "What do you think I should do next year?" This question predictably arises in late August or early September when everyone is embarking on the new school year. Little does she realize that she has an extraordinary influence in the world doing what she has always done—teaching children the love of God. First with our own children and then in Bible-study fellowship, she plants seeds that grow under God's watchful eyes but may be invisible to us mortals.

As a children's study leader, she pores over her Bible diligently and then must decide how to translate those truths into a language that a four year old can understand, not to mention keep up with them physically. Ever try to explain Cain and Abel to four-year-old Billy while simultaneously dancing with hyperactive Sally and monitoring Jill as she goes to the potty? How about bringing the concept of grace and mercy down to the four-year-old level? Talk about being gifted! These are talents only God can appreciate. Yet she feels insecure in telling other people what she does for a ministry.

Frequently we hear prospective short-term–mission team members similarly question (or complain) that they simply aren't gifted for service in a foreign land or culture. I've seen electricians, plumbers, computer software experts, accountants, and virtually every other job portrayed as a skill entirely unneeded on the mission field. In the summer of 1990, our church returned to Guatemala to continue medical ministries, evangelism, and construction. It took a little persuasion on my part to convince the plumbers and electricians that their services would be helpful. Indeed, what a blessing to see the youth on the team learn to pour concrete flooring and to grasp the finer points of simple masonry. We even noted the inevitable competition (culture transferred directly from the United States, of course) with Rebecca telling Aaron after completing work on the floors of two rooms in a new chapel, "The girls' concrete floor is smoother than the boys'!"

But our computer expert, Scott, seemed unconvinced that he would be of any use in a Third-World setting. We tried ineffectively to emphasize his role as an adult counselor. He was a computer man through and through. And he questioned if his airfare was going to be wasted. "Why not get another cook or recruit another youth pastor?" he repeatedly asked. But he went because he knew that in some strange manner he was called. And when we arrived in Guatemala City, his faith was further tested. His allergies were quite well controlled in Seattle, but whatever the offending pollen, it was in full force in this part of Central America. His red nose could have been a beacon for arriving aircraft. Why was he here?

Then he received word that an emergency had occurred back at home. His wife had urgently taken their son, Billy, to the hospital with a fever and abdominal pain. Fortunately, we were still in Guatemala City and had not yet gone out to the villages, so communication was possible. We heard that the diagnosis was appendicitis and that Billy had gone into surgery. Wasn't this just another sign that God had no purpose for him here in Guatemala? Fitfully he awaited news about the outcome of the operation. He paced the floor. Should he return to the states? His wife had told him that the rest of the family was okay and that Billy was already in the operating room, but should he try to grab a quick flight back to Seattle? That was the problem. There are no "quick flights" to Seattle from Guatemala City. If he caught a plane, he would be out of communication for six to eight of the next twelve hours. By then, the operation would be over. So he waited and prayed.

Fortunately, it was simple appendicitis. The operation was uncomplicated, and Billy was in the recovery room and awake within two hours. Then he was faced with another decision. Should he return to help his wife with the other two children and to comfort Billy during his recovery? But by now he had begun to feel an unusual sense of calling to this place, and the entire congregation back home would help Sally. A difficult decision, but he stayed with the team. Still, he wasn't really sure why.

Over the next few days as the team began the medical ministry, Scott explored the YWAM base and discovered that the administrative and financial books were a perfect example of chaos. No one knew how to use the computers, let alone repair the broken ones. They needed connection technology, hard drive de-fragmenting, re-installation of some software, and instruction in operation in some of the bookkeeping programs. Worst of all, they didn't even know that they needed any of this work. It took only a fraction of a day for Scott to discover that a computer expert really could be useful in a developing country.

Soon he couldn't tear himself away from his work. Lunch would come and go with Scott poring over the hardware manuals surrounded by pieces of computer lying all over the table. When it came time for the youth group to go further into the mountains for some medical clinics with the doctors and nurses, Scott asked politely if he could stay behind to finish the job that he now knew God had called him to accomplish. And some of the computers are still being used today, over ten years after his labors.

Another member of the same team had similar problems developing a vision for his place in God's geography. Patrick was an electrical engineer. Not an electrician, an electrical engineer. He designed intricate components for electrical systems and often referred to himself as a propeller head, an engineer's fond self-description that is equivalent to a computer nerd calling himself a geek or techie. He envisioned his knowledge as useless on the mission field, too esoteric, and not practical enough. However, he chose to go to Guatemala to support the youth group. Knowing little about the needs on the YWAM base, he decided simply to be a chaperone for the team. His first encounter with the base's physical plant was literally shocking. Edgard, the base leader, asked him to survey some of the electrical system because the circuit breakers had been tripping a lot. The first discovery was the ungrounded electrical water heaters in the men's dormitory.

For those of you who have never seen a Central American water heater, the entire system is built into the showerhead. It simply heats the water as it passes through the pipe to drench the person below. It avoids heating the water in a tank before use and has the efficiency of only heating the water being used at the moment, at least in theory. In practice, it warms the water only slightly, taking the frigid edge off the temperature. A faulty, ungrounded showerhead bears a striking resemblance to the head cap of an electric chair. The latter alternative was what Patrick found in the shower stall. These ungrounded and malfunctioning heaters were responsible for both tripping the circuit breaker (thank you, God, at least for a functioning circuit breaker) and tingling the unsuspecting YWAMer in the cool of morning. (They were wondering why the devotions had been particularly scintillating recently.)

Patrick's next discovery was in the yard of the YWAM base complex. As he followed some of the power lines through the "conduits" in the ground, he discovered that they not only had no conduits, but in places, they had no insulation. Another reason for the current leaks and increasing budgetary needs for purchasing fuses for the system. It was not only inefficient but also potentially dangerous. So Patrick's job was also providentially defined. The next week he repaired and grounded all showerheads and replaced some live wires in the ground. He had expected to be a useless appendage on the trip but discovered that he was the only person around who understood the basics of electrical wiring. It was not exactly a feat of engineering wizardry, but preventing a missionary from electrocution is not too shabby an accomplishment.

Same team, still in Guatemala, we had another skeptic about his potential to impact a ministry. Peter is a construction logistics expert. In the States, he arranges the coordination of building projects. He lines up the materials and makes sure that the right men are at the right places at the right times. He too went to Guatemala skeptical about his role. Was he to cook meals, to drive a bus, or to lead devotions in the morning? Certainly he would be unable to use his skills in Guatemala; he couldn't even speak Spanish. But he was obedient to what he felt was a call to the church's short-term mission. It wasn't for his children's sake, for they were too young to go. His wife was supportive, but she wasn't going either. Still Peter persisted, and before he knew it, he found himself in the midst of strange intonations calling, "Hermano (Brother) Peter."

At first, the experience was both perplexing and frustrating. Working on the YWAM base took all of his tolerance because it seemed that nothing was ever accomplished on time. Interminable delays were the rule, not the exception. The concept of "Guatemala time" was exasperating. Nothing started when it was scheduled, and nothing was finished on time. After he arrived in Guatemala, he learned that the base team was constructing a new chapel. It was simple in construction—

cinderblock and cement with minimal woodwork. The roof was made of corrugated material. None of this construction should have required much organizational skill, but Peter discovered that the menial task of obtaining the cinderblock could take weeks, and the team had neglected preparation to have the materials on hand. The youth team was only to be in Guatemala for three weeks, and the materials had not even been ordered.

Peter's first attempt to bring the system into North-American order brought him to his knees. He sent Tom to the hardware store to purchase a hacksaw blade the first morning about 9:00. He was ready to call out for the police when 5:00 p.m. rolled around and Tom had still not returned. As dinner was being completed, Tom straggled into the base, looking like he was ready to return to the good ol' U.S. of A. It had consumed nine hours to accomplish the simple task of finding the blade (the hard part) and purchasing it (not as easy as it sounds), with a few added hours of traveling to and from countless stores in Guatemala City to find what was needed.

Peter knew that he had met his match. Building a skyscraper in Seattle was a piece of cake compared to constructing a simple cinderblock chapel in Guatemala. What he learned as he coordinated this effort was that Central Americans don't just work toward finishing a task. They build friendships in the process. Sure it can be difficult to locate a hacksaw blade in Guatemala City, but one doesn't rush to buy it when the elusive item is found. You talk with the shopkeeper. You learn about his children. You hear about his wife's recent operation. You build relationships. And you walk away with both a hacksaw blade and a new friend. And that new friend just might come to church with you next Sunday. And who knows what after that? So Peter indeed built a chapel. It wasn't totally complete by the time he boarded the airplane to go home, but he had a neighborhood of new friends—the man who sells hacksaw blades, the concrete salesman, the local expert in roofing, the nail salesman at the hardware store, and many others, some of whom became real brothers in Christ in the process. Peter learned patience. Peter learned relationships. And Peter discovered who God wanted him to be in just three weeks.

Transport yourself to Honduras in 1987. Different country, different year, but the same dilemma. Paula is a hairdresser from California. She had sensed a leading to join a group ministering in the wilds of La Mosquitia—the swampy, northeastern portion of Honduras. She hadn't a clue about her role in the ministry there. The team was a medical brigade, dispatched to combat some very unhealthy conditions. (It's no secret why they call the region La Mosquitia. Malaria and dengue fever dominate the illnesses there, not to mention tropical skin diseases, gastrointestinal ailments from impure water, injuries from fighting among the local political rivals, and cholera.) What did a hairdresser know about any of these things? But the major reason for the group to be there was, of course, to show the love of God.

Paula thought that she didn't fit in. God had a different assessment of her role, however. After about three weeks of medical ministry, Paula had learned a bit about administering medicines and telling the local women how to purify their water. But the nearest local village seemed resistant to any of this activity. And the people there didn't accept the "gringos." But Paula had a plan. She did what she knew best—she offered to give the women in the village a beauty treatment free of charge. The response was overwhelming. They came to her like mosquitoes in the heat at dusk. Everyone wanted her attention. No one had ever given a woman in this village a haircut and beauty treatment, let alone such personalized attention. Does God care about out personal appearance? Yes, but not to the extent that He cares about our souls. Paula's attention was translated across the language barrier as "caring" and "personal dignity." After the beauty treatments, the women wanted to know why the team was near their village, and why a fair-skinned Californian would come to the swamp in 105-plus degree heat to take care of their hair. Her simple gift to them opened the door for the gospel. Planned by Paula? No. Planned by God? Yes, of course. A simple servant was willing to give from what she had. She reaped what she had dreamed for a God whom she loved.

So if you think you are called to a short-term mission trip but don't know if your skills and talents can be used, worry no longer. Remember that Matthew 28 already defines the job: "Therefore go and make disciples of all nations, baptizing them in the name of the Father and of the Son and of the Holy Spirit, and teaching them to obey everything I have commanded you. And surely I am with you always, to the very end of the age" Matthew 28:19-20.

Your only duty is to be faithful. God will provide and show you your role in the process. You can pray, give, or go. Or do two of the above. Or all three.

However, organizing a mission trip can evoke enthusiasm rather than reveal a calling. Enthusiasm alone is not enough, particularly for youth groups where team emotion can cause everyone to want to go when only a select few may be called. Our youth pastor has created a mechanism to help him and the elders of the church discern who should go. A panel of members of the church, often composed mostly of parents of the youth, interviews the prospective team members, asking them probing questions to help them discern who goes (see Appendix D).

So who should go on a mission trip? Anyone who is called by God, and God calls all of us. The only issue is the destination. Paul writes, "But you will receive power when the Holy Spirit comes on you; and you will be my witnesses in Jerusalem, and in all Judea and Samaria, and to the ends of the earth" (Acts 1:8).

Not all are called to a *foreign* field. Some are supposed to witness at only home. All are called to pray, and all are called to tithe. Some are also called to give additional financial support to the cause. But who goes? Quietly waiting upon God in prayer is one answer to the question. We have many clues at our disposal such as

- Scripture,
- prayer,
- confirmation from other believers, and
- circumstances.

Notice that feelings should only be a minor aspect of your calling. Acts 20:22 explains the calling. We must be

- compelled or "pressed in." We should sense God saying that He wants us to go and be unhappy at the thought of staying behind.
- specifically called. Our destination should be a concrete call to a people, a region, or a task.
- going without knowing. The details do not need to be specified, nor do all of the logistics need to be defined before we answer the call. Not all risks are removed, but you still accept the call.
- willing to endure hardships. In spite of the dangers or inconveniences, we still are compelled to go.
- willing to sacrifice. Life is worth nothing compared to the calling. We have little attachment to the world and its goods.
- going to testify. Spreading the good news is the

goal.
* going to complete a task. This trip is not a vacation or sightseeing trip. It has a distinct purpose.

If your prospective mission trip fulfills these criteria, you must go. Staying home is not an option. Life is safer and more rewarding in the uttermost parts of the earth than at home. And perhaps this trip will be the first step in a life of service in a foreign land.

3

"Are blessings free?"

WHAT WILL IT COST?

June 1
Greetings from Balfate!

Today I took Dave and Becky Drozek and their family to La Ceiba for their return to the States. The day started with a few glitches, however. Just before breakfast, one of the doors in the house refused to open, and we had to take it off its hinges to find the rock (actually a seashell) that was keeping it from moving. No big deal. But just as we were about to leave the house, Dave shouted, "Oh, no! We have a big problem." The back rooms of the house were covered with water and a strangely unpleasant odor. The septic system had overflowed and was backing up into the house. (The Drozek's is one of the few houses in Balfate with a septic system—the others have outhouses and no kitchen plumbing.) We quickly turned off all of the water and grabbed two mops, furiously trying to keep the flood from spreading. After about an hour, the floor was reasonably dry, which is not to say pleasant smelling.

41

We then turned to the task of finding the septic tank. Dave and Becky have only lived one year in this thirty-year-old house, so they were not too sure about the logistics of the flow of things, if you get my drift. We located a suspiciously green portion of grass, but by then we had to leave to get to town on time. There are no septic tank cleaners or pumpers in Balfate or anywhere close. Guess what job we have tomorrow? Such is the practice of medicine in Honduras, only slightly more distasteful than filling out insurance forms, however. The rivers were up slightly from last night's rain, but we made it without drowning the Land Cruiser. In town all was peaceful, and we accomplished all of our errands.

WARNING! Medical talk approaching! Abandon hope all ye who read further!

Yesterday we saw an example in clinic of why unrestricted over-the-counter drugs in other countries are bad. A woman came to clinic who had been having some (apparently rather minor) arthritis pain. She had heard that steroids were good for you, so she bought some prednisone in the pharmacy in the big city (no prescription needed). Her arthritis felt better, but when she tried to stop the medication, the pain returned, only worse. She took ever-increasing doses over the years, and by the time we saw her, she had serious Cushing's syndrome—huge weight gain, moon facies, hypertension, edema, severe proximal muscle weakness, and renal damage. We are trying to taper the steroids and replace them with other effective, but non-toxic, medications. Holding our collective breath as we decrease the dose of prednisone.

Whew! Glad that medical mumbo-jumbo is over!

The four-year-old girl with the asthma and pneumonia I mentioned in the last e-mail came back to the clinic yesterday for follow up. Much better! Still some wheezes, but the pneumonia had improved, fever down, etc. She looked like a different little girl. As Clint Eastwood said (under other circumstances), "Go ahead! Make my day!"

Yesterday I made one of those gringo-doesn't-know-the language goofs in clinic. The word for "ham" is jamon, and the word for "soap" is jabon. I told a patient to be sure to wash her hands with a lot of jamon. She wasn't impressed.

June 2

Today we spent part of the day sorting through donations that were given to the hospital and shipped to Balfate over the last year. All of the equipment had to be tested. Unfortunately many (most) are useless. We had twelve suction machines, and not a single one both had all of its parts and worked! Folks seem to donate their junk without thinking that in Central America it will not only be junk but junk without replacement parts. Many items had been manufactured in the '80's. Not as old as I am, but in many respects less useful. (Is that really possible?) Many of the companies have gone out of business.

Here's an occupational hazard that we don't encounter often in the good ol' U.S. of A.: I was looking at a donated ECG machine (circa 1492—Chris did a few cardiograms on the boat coming to America), when I discovered a wasps' nest inside it. I certainly would have been stung by the results of that test!

It is truly amazing what was in some of the boxes: (1) a sack full of metal clothes hangers (Let's see, we could straighten them out and use them for catheter introducers.); (2) a Richland, Ohio, telephone book—yellow pages included, of course (Never know when *you'll need to call from Central America for a pizza. Does the thirty-minute delivery guarantee still hold?); (3) a sack full of very large corks ("Open wide and say 'Ahhh'!"); and too many others to mention.*

I'm sorry if the descriptions above seem ungrateful. I know that many people want to help the poor, but I become angry when I see the trash given to missionaries. Why not give them the best and keep some of the clothes with holes in them at home? Speaking of which: Shop Wal-Mart! Wal-Mart sent a local missionary in La Ceiba about 3,500 pounds (really!) of new clothes to distribute to the poor, and the shipment arrived yesterday. I saw the fifty-plus boxes in his home when I took the Drozeks to the airport. That's worthy of a spending spree at your local Wal-Mart. Tell the manager, "Thank you!" Yeah, it wasn't his personal decision to make the donation, but he deserves the feedback, anyway.

By the way, I'm blissfully entrenched in Phase 3 of the life of a short-term missionary—wet and dirty (and hot) and not caring too much about it.

You're probably thinking, "This guy has too much time on his hands if he can write so much." Not true except at night. Quite an empty house. Only ten days, twenty-three hours, and five minutes until Judy and Matt arrive. But who's counting? No doubt my letters will shrink when Judy and Matt arrive and as my stay here becomes longer.

No time for the septic system today. We'll sniff that one out tomorrow.

June 3
The sweet non-smell of success! Septic system is working again. Enough said.

I spent the rest of my Saturday writing lists of drugs to be purchased for the emergency care area of the clinic, and I began to write treatment protocols for various emergencies. At night, I went over to the O'Neils' house for dinner (not starving yet, though if I try to look even more pathetic than I already am, I may get invited back). We played Monopoly until the wee hours (around here, the wee hours are from 7:00 to 9:00 p.m.).

The night was punctuated by the cat awakening me about ten times or more to play games. Fortunately, she has been declawed. She just seems distressed that the house is so empty. Her name is Midnight, and that's about when the games began. Tomorrow, I'll try closing the bedroom door.

June 4

We went to church this morning—a different one from last Tuesday. It is a Baptist mission church, and the pastor spoke more clearly and slowly. I could understand a bit more.

The day actually started with the power going out at 6:00 a.m. The power has been out at least once a day since I arrived. Usually it is only off a few minutes. Today it was out for about ten hours. It gave me the chance to learn to use the generator (and to realize that fans are a great luxury!).

Speaking of luxuries, it's amazing how one savors a prized food in Central America. I brought a bag of M&Ms from the states where we usually gobble a handful at a time. Here I eat one at a time, slowly. The favorite that we take for granted elsewhere becomes a true experience in Honduras. The United States is a handful-of-M&Ms-at-a-time country; Honduras is a one-M&M-at-a-time country.

June 5

For the second day in a row, I saw a person with a goiter the size of an orange or at least two large kumquats. (Why do we always measure something by the size of a fruit or sports equipment, such as "big as a baseball"?) No tests available. (Medical folks, that means no TSH, no T4, no T3, no scan, no x-rays, no ultrasound, etc.) What's a person to do? Send her to town? She walked four hours to get here. The costs of the tests would exceed her family's annual income! So we do the best we can without tests. Give her thyroid hormone and pray that she doesn't get worse. Of course, she had many other problems as well.

The best part of my day was that when one of my patients got up to leave, he hugged me for being here to help him. I think that's very unusual here in this culture. All of you back in the States who are supporting us in any way, consider yourself hugged by Juan!

Dinner last night was beans and potatoes. Tonight I thought that I'd have a little variety (always living on the wild side of life, hovering precariously close to the edge), so I had potatoes and beans.

June 6

Today I had my first experience with a machete wound. A nine-year-old boy came to clinic from his school. Children are required to do the upkeep on the schoolyard, and the upkeep is performed with a machete. He got a little too close to his neighbor, who was also wielding a machete, and wound up with a two to three inch gash on his left arm. Fortunately, it was not too deep. It's been a long time since I have *played with 4-0 silk sutures, but it's just like riding a bicycle . . . almost.*

In the evening, Pad O'Neil, Buddy Dodson, and I walked over some land that is going to be developed for housing long-term missionaries and for future use by the hospital. It is a crucial piece of land with access needed for some of the hospital activities. Earlier in the day, the owner, Don Santiago, had told Pad and Buddy that he would not sell it. Pad and Buddy felt strangely peaceful about it, even though the small piece of land was desperately needed. They simply went to a hilltop overlooking it and prayed. About an hour later, the owner came back to them and told them that he had not changed his mind. He still would not sell it—he wanted to give it to them instead. Now that's an answer to prayer with a plus!

June 7

The word for the day today was "improvise." Can you spell "improvise?" A man came to the clinic who had severed an Achilles' tendon eight weeks ago. He and a "friend" had become embroiled in a drunken brawl, and, you guessed it, began going at each other with machetes. Our patient had his right Achilles' tendon cut, and Dr. Dave repaired it and put his lower leg in a cast. He returned today, eight weeks later, to have the cast removed. One problem. We don't have a cast cutter or cast saw. So we went to the machine shop at the hospital. Screwdriver? No. Chainsaw? No. Crowbar? No. Finally we found some tin snips. Viola! Cast removed! The wound was more than a little infected. ("Keep it clean and dry" doesn't translate into the life and work of the Honduran men.) So we cleaned the wound, removed the skin stitches, and gave him some antibiotics. We'll see in a few days if it is going to heal.

We saw three folks today who could have used an ultrasound (two abdomen, one heart), but it is not available here yet. Another needed an MRI (really!), but as they say, "Only in your dreams!" Gotta keep reminding myself, "Just do what you can do. God will provide the rest."

June 8

Enrico is a laborer. He spent some years in the States but returned to Honduras a few years ago. Six days ago, he was walking in the mountains and, feeling energetic, he started to jog downhill. He caught his foot in the root of a mango tree, and fell, rolling downhill. His knee hurt him greatly, but his custom is to "tough it out" because it is so difficult to get medical care in this part of Honduras. After four days and persistent swelling in the left knee, he came to our clinic, walking three miles to get here. Our diagnosis was a tear of the medial meniscus. No x-rays, no MRI, just a clinical exam. Fortunately a visiting physical therapist at the clinic that day helped us, and he outlined a plan for him, gave him crutches, some medicines, and told him that he must stay off his feet for a few days. But Enrico has no savings, no disability insurance, no food put away in the cupboard, and no one else in the family to do his job as a welder—no way to survive except to work. I saw him today, welding as usual, hobbling around using crutches when he could but mostly not. Such is life in Honduras. Almost everyone here is an Enrico.

June 9

Today a regional healthcare worker walked to our clinic and reviewed for us the principles of malaria control. Actually there is just one principle: If the patient has chills and fever that you can't explain, it's malaria. Pretty simple. Everyone with chills and fever without an obvious cause is supposed to get five days of malaria medication—chloroquine and primaquine. The patient also gets a blood smear for malaria sent to the big city for analysis. If it is positive for malaria parasites, the healthcare worker returns to make sure that the person did okay (it takes a month or two). He also warned us about an epidemic of leishmaniasis around here. It is transmitted by the bite of a certain kind of insect. (Makes my legs itch just to think about it.) Guess I'll have to read up more on that one. He reassured me that my tick bites now are not too dangerous. There's no lyme disease here and supposedly no rickettsial diseases either.

There's a small library in the clinic. I saw the least used book this afternoon hiding on the upper shelf: The Complete Guide to Medicare Regulations.

Yesterday another missionary came to town for a visit and asked us to join him at "the finest restaurant in Balfate." We quickly accepted. It is called Maribel's and is both the finest and the worst restaurant in town—it's the only restaurant. It used to have two pool tables in one end, but now it has a pulperia (a small convenience store with a couple dozen items) at that end. Maribel is a very nice woman who sometimes can be a bit abrupt. After we sat for a few minutes, she came over and said rather emphatically, "Pollo!" ("Chicken!") I was informed that she usually has two items: chicken and fish, both deep fried. Today there was no fish, so the menu choices were either fried chicken or fried chicken. In fact it, was very good (okay, deep fried isn't exactly the way the American Heart

Association prefers food to be cooked, but you don't argue with Maribel).

June 10
   Question: What does a cardiologist in Honduras do on a Saturday? Answer: Just what he does in the States, as little as possible. I did a few repairs around the house (don't worry, Dave and Becky, I didn't break anything). Did the laundry. Washed a few windows. The usual.

   Today it only got up to 98 degrees—a cool spell brought in with the rain. And last night it got down to 83. Not exactly Seattle.

   It's interesting how your survival instincts kick in when you're on your own. Did you know that there are 307 ways to make peanut butter and jelly sandwiches? And the broiled spaghetti is a work of art. But my pièce de résistance (that's French, not Spanish) is macaroni and cheese a la cantaloupe. Yum, yum. Judy and Matt arrive in three more days (God willing and assuming TACA Airlines behaves unusually and actually delivers a flight on time). Not a minute too soon. I'm sure that I heard the cat talking to me today.

   I am really out of my comfort zone here. This week I did pediatrics, gynecology, orthopedics, dermatology, general internal medicine, endocrinology, ENT, GI, ophthalmology, pulmonary medicine, and mostly infectious disease. Only a teeny bit of cardiology. Question: How many cardiologists does it take to examine a baby? Answer: Two. One to do the exam and the other one to read the how-to book.

   The people here are really precious. They walk three to eight hours just to get to the clinic, wait six hours in the "waiting room," and then are grateful for their ten minutes or so with a gringo who speaks very little Spanish. May we take instruction from them in patience and tolerance! The waiting room, by the way, is called the Sala de Espera. (Espera means wait, but esperar means to hope, so it could also be called the "room of hope," quite a humbling thought to this gringo.)

June 11

Another random thought: I noticed that the term here for "housewife" is ama de casa, which literally means lover of the house. It certainly gives more honor to women of the home than we confer upon them in the States.

Today as I was in church, I was really happy that I understood the first two-thirds of the sermon, but the pastor had more words than time, so his word-per-minute count went way up in the last third of the lesson. I sure hope that there was nothing important in that last third because I missed most of it (unfortunately, it's probably like the Final Four in basketball where most of the action occurs). Maybe by the end of our time here I'll be able to follow the pastoral final third.

June 12

(Somebody's birthday, I think, but I can't remember whose.)

The Drozeks have a fan in the attic that runs on a thermostat. It comes on when it's hot. Last night was the first time in over two weeks that it turned itself off.

Today as I was driving to the clinic, which is about four miles from the town of Balfate itself, two women hailed the car and asked for a ride. One was in her *mid-fifties, and she lovingly helped her tiny eighty-five-year-old mother into the car. I truly don't know how they expected the older woman to walk all of that distance. She was hobbling slowly on arthritic knees and breathing heavily from her lung congestion. They told me that they had to get to the clinic because they had heard that a heart doctor was in town, and they thought that Mom needed to see a heart doctor. She had never seen any kind of a doctor, let alone a heart doctor.*

I gave them the ride and dropped them off at the line of people waiting for the opening of the clinic. Then I went into the clinic myself. About five hours later, it was their turn, and I said hello to them again. She has valvular heart disease, though obviously her valves have served her well for eighty-five years. After an exam, an EKG, a complex set of new medicines, and about thirty minutes of time, she was ready to go. I told her I'd see her in a week, and she told me that she wanted God to bless me for being there. Then I got a hug from a four foot, eleven inch giant.

What is the cost of a short-term mission trip? I've briefly outlined the financial cost. What's the cost in terms of dedication, time, and emotion? And where should you go?

Knowing where to go presents no problem for most churches. Nearly all churches support at least one missionary either directly or indirectly. Learning which ones need the particular help or skills possessed by members of your team may become clear as you look at the roster of missionaries you support. In fact, it is more common that you know who needs support and the real question is "Who should participate in this particular endeavor?" Praying for God to match the site with people may take some time and effort, however.

For churches without direct connections to missionaries on the field, and especially for youth groups that may need more structure, there are many parachurch mission agencies that organize trips for church groups or even for individuals (such as Youth With A Mission, Teen Challenge, and Operation Mobilization—see Appendix H). Most denominational mission boards also have programs that their congregations can utilize.

Knowing where to go and then actually achieving a safe arrival at the intended destination can be quite distinct tasks. On my first trip to Honduras, I had great difficulty meeting up with my team. They were scheduled to go into the jungle by way of a treacherous and convoluted journey on a public bus, then on a conveyance called a *burra*, which is a small railroad car pushed along flat land by a strong Honduran, then in a canoe down a long river, and finally by hiking through a snake- and iguana-infested jungle. My communication with the team had been spotty at best, and I waited alone for three days in La Ceiba hoping to meet up with them to foray into the jungle.

At one point, a friendly (perhaps too friendly) person near my hotel offered to take me to the destination village, Colorado Barra. My immediate response was one of suspicion. This man could get me into the jungle and handily steal everything I had, or worse. I politely declined. On the fourth day, I was sitting in a cafe on the edge of the town square when I heard a voice behind me, "Are you Leon?" I knew from the Australian accent that my team had found me. It was Andrew Wark, the Aussie leading the YWAM team.

The next morning we embarked on the trip into the

jungle, and it remains one of my most memorable experiences. We saw beautiful birds, clear skies, gorgeous foliage, and fruit sufficient to remind us of the Garden of Eden. As we rode the railroad pushcarts through the dense brush, we sat on the old flat, wooden surfaces, picked mangoes off the passing branches, and had a feast as if God had told us, "Here. This is my bounty for you. Eat and be filled."

We had another experience that convinced us that not all missionaries should host visiting teams. We first discovered this principle on a trip to Honduras in 1989. The youth pastor, Steve Allen, and I went to Tegucigalpa in December to investigate an opportunity for our youth group the next summer. It's crucial to the success of a mission trip that the leadership of your church knows the destination well and that your team has a trustworthy missionary to guide your activities there. We had been told that a mission in Tegucigalpa had a remote outpost that was laboring to develop sustainable agricultural projects near a large lake in the center of the country. When we got there, we were met at the airport by a man who reminded us of a cross between a Texan, a marine, and an escaped convict. He wore large boots and a cowboy hat, had a gun rack in his pickup, and drove like someone was chasing him.

Neither Steve nor I had thought ourselves to be blessed with the gift of discernment, but immediately upon meeting this man, we looked at each other and thought, "Let's get out of here. Now!" However, we were stuck. In a foreign country with no notion of where to go for food or shelter, we were compelled to go with him to his home. It was lavish. Opulent. Clearly not a good witness to the poor masses around him. And in the bedroom where we stayed the night, we discovered some boxes at the foot of our two beds that suggested a connection with less-than-virtuous organizations in the United States.

After a fitful night's sleep, we were poorly prepared for the three-hour ride to the agricultural project the next morning. Our host seemed compelled to make the ride into a two-hour horror movie. He drove like the wind, and we feared reaping the whirlwind. Often we had to remind him to stop looking at us when talking and to keep his eyes on the road. He seemed determined to avoid all of the potholes in the road, an impossible task in Central America. Weaving from side to side, he avoided wear-and-tear on the tires by keeping two of them in the air. Both Steve and I were physical wrecks by the time we arrived at the mission outpost. Never mind, however.

We had no opportunity to interact with the missionaries because our host and the family at the station spent the next few hours talking about the problems being encountered on the field. We simply prayed for our safety on the return trip, which was no less an adventure.

The next day we graciously declined any further tours of this ministry. Clearly we could not trust the hosts to provide for the safety and ministry of our youth group. Had we not visited the site prior to the proposed trip, we could have exposed our team to great spiritual peril as well as physical danger. The cost of such a mission trip could have been the life of one of our youth. This mission organization was less than marginal, and we prayed that they would not ruin the witness of any other Christian groups working in the area. This experience taught us that not all missionaries are virtuous, and some are just as troubled as many Christians in the United States.

The preceding story does not mean that we are to

seek opportunities only where it is comfortable and safe. We need to prayerfully seek where God would have us serve as well as do our homework and investigate all aspects of the mission program.

One of the most rewarding mission trips I ever joined was a medical relief trip to Rwanda in 1994. It occurred at the height of the refugee crisis during the bloodiest part of the civil war between the Hutus and the Tutsis, a conflict that has been raging for over 400 years. In Goma, Zaire, nearly 10,000 refugees were dying daily, mostly from cholera. Our team's motto came from Psalm 91,"You will not fear the terror of night, nor the arrow that flies by day, nor the pestilence that stalks in the darkness, nor the plague that destroys at midday. A thousand may fall at your side, ten thousand at your right hand, but it will not come near you" (Psalm 91:5–7).

Our leader, Doug Nichols, prepared us by saying, "God called us to minister here. He never said we'd come back alive." Our trip there was like a scene out of a B-grade movie. Once in Zaire, in order to complete our journey to the center of Africa, we boarded a decrepit 707 that had long since exceeded its useful lifespan, followed by a trip on the worst maintained 737 I have ever seen. The 707 had no seats, let alone seatbelts. We stretched out on bags of beans and rice. The only person with a seatbelt was sitting in a car, which was being transported, in the center of the airplane. And when it got cold at the high altitude, the person started the car to turn on the heater (until we reminded him that the exhaust fumes might incapacitate the pilot). The tires on the later flight, the 737, were threadbare, the lights didn't work, the ventilation system was non-existent, and forget about using the on-board toilet. Fortunately the captain flew like a fighter pilot, so we had no time to think about the condition of the airplane, just to hold on tight and pray.

At one stop, we were asked to leave the plane for a few minutes, and some of our team was taken to a small room in the airport for interrogation. We learned quickly that we should never let anyone go anywhere alone. Always go in two's or three's for safety.

God calls us where we will be useful, not where we will be comfortable. And there we are to serve. God is the provider, in spite of His servants.

What is the cost of a mission trip? Sometimes fear and uncertainty. On one trip to eastern Honduras in 1988, the pilot for Mission Aviation Fellowship was ferrying a team of six people to a remote area where there were no roads. What is a runway for such pilots? Any segment of flat land with no trees or cows. He made the trip twice in the four-place Cessna 172, and as he began to depart our mission clinic the second time, we were a bit apprehensive about whether he would return to retrieve us a month later. He wrote our team name in a small spiral notebook and stuffed it into his pocket. As he boarded the plane, we pleaded, "Don't lose that little book!"

What is the cost of a mission trip? Sometimes mental distress and the confrontation of spiritual depravity. North Korea was the darkest country I have ever visited on any short-term mission trip; it was even worse than India. Our group from Northwest Medical Teams was invited by the North Korean government to visit the country and to assess the medical system, which was in shambles. To this day, I'm still not really sure why they invited us to come. I think it was to begin to seek help from the outside world since they were in the midst of widespread starvation and their medical system was near complete annihilation.

Whatever their reasons, four of us went for three

weeks touring the country, teaching, and delivering medical supplies to the areas hardest hit by the poverty. Our every move was scripted and monitored. From the instant we stepped off the airplane, a "guide" accompanied us. Even at night, if we wanted to take a walk around the neighborhood of our hotel, a guide just happened to be nearby, wanting to take a walk also.

One day the team leader, Dr. John Park, was talking to the guide when he mentioned Dr. Park's sister. Dr. Park stopped the discussion abruptly and said, "I never told you I had a sister." The guide, nonplussed, said with steely eyes, "I know everything about you. That's my job." Immediately we knew that they had researched our backgrounds. What else did they know about us? Later in the week, Dr. Park had a tearful reunion with this sister when we went to the south of the North Korean countryside where she lived. It was a touching scene because they had not seen each other for almost ten years.

After we left North Korea and were back in Beijing, Dr. Park asked the three of us if we had noticed anything unusual about their meeting. We commented that it was very touching to see them reunited after so many years. He seemed relieved, and he then told us that she had traveled a great distance to his hotel room in secret a few nights earlier because they didn't know if the authorities would actually let them meet later in the week. She had hid in the back of a truck under a blanket, knowing that she would be arrested if found because she did not have a visa to travel into Pyongyang, where we were staying. (A citizen of North Korea cannot travel freely, and a visa is required even to go to another city.) When she arrived at the hotel, she bribed the desk clerk to allow her to go to her brother's room. However, after only five minutes, the clerk changed his mind and came to whisk her back to the truck. So when the two of them met later in the week, they had to pretend that they had not seen each other for many years, fearing that if the authorities became suspicious, she would be in trouble. The ruse worked, and their second reunion looked like it was their first.

The entire trip in North Korea was precisely scripted. We had the opportunity to go to church twice while we were there. We were told that churches were allowed in North Korea, but we soon learned that only two tiny churches existed for the 3 million people in Pyongyang— one Catholic and one Protestant. We were first asked which church we would like to attend, as though we had a choice. Because our team leader was Catholic, we said, "Catholic this week, Protestant next." But we were quickly told that we would attend the Protestant church this week. (I guess they had hoped that we would choose the Protestant so it would look like we had been given freedom of choice.)

Turns out, both church services had been planned and scripted for us. The "members" of the church were apparently handpicked, and they attended whenever a visiting group was in town (not often). Blissfully unaware of this scripting, we were happy to go to the little Protestant church. It seemed a bit unusual that the church service had already started by the time we arrived, but initially we gave it no thought. The minister told us that Billy Graham had visited this church years ago, and we listened to the sermon through the translation of our team leader. After a while, we noted that our leader was translating very few words, and tears came to his eyes. He told us that the "minister" was not really preaching anything from the Bible, but that he was extolling the virtues of Kim Il Sung and Kim Jong Il, the recently deceased leader and his son who had taken over power about two years previously. A political speech was all that was allowed in church. Then they escorted us out as the choir was singing the final hymn. We were told that we had to get to our next meeting, so the entire experience was tainted by the control of our political guides.

The next week, we were allowed to go to the Catholic church, but a similar scene emerged. All of us were ready to go over an hour before the service was to start. The church was only a couple of miles from our hotel, and there was absolutely no traffic. Nevertheless, we left late and drove about fifteen miles per hour. Needless to say, we arrived after the service had started. This seemed to be a pattern! The church, it turned out, had no priest, and the message was simply a welcome for us, the visiting Americans. After fifteen minutes, we were ushered out the right-hand doors, and the North Koreans exited through the left-hand doors. Now we understood the pattern! We were not to be allowed to speak with the North Koreans (two of our four team members spoke fluent Korean). Even though the congregation was handpicked in these "demonstration churches," they still could not be trusted to talk with us.

We now suspect that the doors to these churches are locked on Sundays when foreign visitors are not present. We asked our handlers if we could visit some home churches, if there were any. They feigned ignorance about any home church movement. We wondered if persecution was causing the underground church to flourish as it had in China.

What is the cost of a mission trip? Sometimes it is intense emotion or even post-traumatic stress. Few memories reliably bring tears to my eyes. Rwanda's orphans are an exception. In the summer of 1994, I was part of a small group of doctors, nurses, and support personnel who found ourselves running a hospital at the extreme eastern edge of the refugee camp named Kibumba. That's where God had determined that we would go. By day we worked in the hospital and clinic; by night we retreated to the nearest town, Goma, Zaire, because it was too dangerous to remain in the camp. The Rwandans had many refugee nurses, so we turned the hospital over to them at night.

Each morning we returned to treat the results of life in the dirty, cramped, and malnourished conditions in which this proud people struggled. Trucks drove daily through the camp, manned by the "boy scouts," as we called them. They were doing the good deed that others refused to consider—collecting the corpses of those who had failed to survive the night. At the peak of the crisis, it is estimated that 10,000 people were dying each day. This figure made our team's theme Bible chapter (Psalm 91) more poignant: "Ten thousand at your right hand."

Our team did not suffer a single serious illness throughout the entire time that we served in this desolate camp. But the 10,000 daily Rwandan deaths—fewer during the last days our team was there—created yet other casualties. Children were left without parents. Many of the children had simply been separated from their parents during the forced exodus from their country into Zaire. The United Nations had a striking euphemism for these orphans; they were called "unaccompanied children." Don't call them orphans—that sounds too harsh. Give them a name that has less emotion attached to it. But the 10,000 deaths occurring daily created real orphans. Friends and acquaintances often tried to take the new orphans into their four-by-six-foot twig and brush tents. However, many times there was simply not enough room or food for them. They became the "leftovers" at the end of the day.

Our daily trip out of the camp was a long, dusty serpentine route back to the main road that led to Goma where we spent the night. Often as we dragged ourselves into our four-wheel-drive vehicle, someone would come to us with an orphan. An infant in this camp would soon die, so we took each day's "leftovers" to an orphanage in the middle of the camp that was run by another aid organization. Holding an infant in our arms as we drove along the rugged road to the orphanage was a heart-wrenching experience for all of us, even for the most hardened of the team. More distressing was the ease of depositing the infants at the orphanage. It was deceptively quick with few questions asked. Just another added to the hundreds already housed there. And years later, many of them probably still know only the sounds present on the inside of a tent, the hunger of refugee rations, and the absence of a relative's hug. They are adding to the tragedy of the orphan crisis created by AIDS in Africa. Leftover children. Here come the tears.

Is the cost worthwhile? Of course!

4

"When all else fails, read the instruction book."

PREPARATION, ARRIVAL, AND CULTURE SHOCK

June 13

Judy and Matt arrived safely after the airplane trip from Sheol. They had a beautiful tour of the United States before coming to Honduras. How's this for an itinerary? Seattle to Denver to Las Vegas to New Orleans to San Pedro Sula to La Ceiba. Thirty-two and a half hours without a break. Don't ask! When they finally arrived, the luggage was missing of course. My Spanish is still a bit shaky, but here is what I understood from the TACA agent in La Ceiba: The bags are being held hostage by a small group of independent pro-mujahadin rebel terrorists in the southwestern corner of Afghanistan, who are conspiring with the Airline Pilots' Association. To redeem the luggage, we have to deliver our firstborn son to Kabul with 16 million dollars in unmarked twenty-dollar bills in a brown paper bag. I think that's what she said.

June 14

Today we drove from La Ceiba to Balfate early

enough to get there for 8:00 a.m. clinic. How early was our departure? Way too.

Clinic was busy with many last minute drop-ins. Just like in the United States, the sickest seem to arrive at the end of the day. One we had to send to La Ceiba to be operated upon...we hope. We'll all be glad when our own hospital is open so we don't have to rely on these perilous "transfers."

When we arrived back at the house at about five that evening, the temperature inside the house was 92 degrees, outside it was 100. Don't know what the high was. Don't want to know.

June 15

I continued setting up the diagnostic lab today. There is much left to be done, but at least now we have the basic tests.

At the end of the afternoon, we heard an airplane flying overhead—an unusual sound out here where the predominant background noise is birds singing, interrupted occasionally by a white-faced monkey screeching. The plane then made a pass over the clinic so low that the wheels nearly opened a new ventilation portal in my room. It was a friend who was flying the proposed approach for a new runway. He reported that there was no way it could work. The runway will need to be more east-west because the north-south approach they had envisioned would require nearly hitting the clinic with any attempted landing pass, even in good weather (this is "good"?).

Judy and Matt are still sleeping quite a bit. No luggage yet, but the rebels in Afghanistan have lowered their demands to one sidewinder surface-to-air missile and three peanut butter sandwiches.

June 16

Today I started with somewhat of a "poor ol' me" mindset. I had twisted a knee, and it was painful to walk. Then a patient came to clinic with a gargantuan knee that had been swollen for two months. The knee was about as big as his upper thigh. He had broken his leg a few years ago, and the metal pin from the previous surgical repair appeared perilously close to the joint space and may have been causing the trouble (he brought with him an X-ray done a few weeks ago elsewhere). So we sent him to town for a surgical consult. Suddenly my knee didn't feel so bad.

Finally as I had been seeing about fifteen patients a day with sore throats and coughs (tos y gripe), I now join their ranks. It instills empathy, so they say. (Just who is "they," anyway?)

Luggage arrived today. It seems to be a pattern— about two or three days after you arrive, your luggage casually strolls onto the scene, like a wayward teenager trying to look cool: "Yo! I'm here. What's the big deal?" The Afghan rebels got only a Snickers candy bar and four old luggage claim checks.

June 17

Today we had a contest. I won. It was a competition to see which would be higher, the ambient afternoon temperature on the porch or my core body temperature. Colds are wonderful; they make you appreciate how good you feel when you don't have one.

Matt is adjusting to the slow pace of life here. A new team arrives from the States in two days to work on the electrical panels for the hospital. He will probably work with them since their team has dwindled from twenty people to six.

WARNING! Anyone who feels compelled to feel sorry for me, read no further!

It is Saturday evening, and we just finished a lovely meal of chicken with a delectable Costa Rican sauce, fresh cucumbers, peppers, and flour tortillas. Now I am listening to a Bob Fitts CD of songs about God comforting His people. The temperature has dropped to a comfortable range after a rather hot afternoon. Outside the sun is setting to my left and in front of me the horses graze in the small pasture between the house and the Caribbean Sea. The young foal tenderly approaches the gate at the end of the driveway, and Coco (the resident dog) and the foal touch noses. They're good friends. The breeze wafts gently off the sea, and the waves crash against the beach in the distance. The moon slowly rises to my right. The music says, "I'll never leave you or forsake you." Sounds right to me.

June 18

I had to miss church this morning because my coughing and sneezing were nearly non-stop (the only non-stop anything we've experienced recently). Judy and Matt went with the O'Neils to the Baptist church established about fifteen years ago by missionaries from the States. They enjoyed it, though many of the finer points of the sermon passed them by.

A young boy came to the gate of the house this afternoon. He said that he had no home, no parents, and that he wanted an empty box to put his clothes in. Being of the suspicious, but not too discerning, type, I questioned the truth of his allegations. He was riding quite a nice dirt bike. He also wanted some treatment for a skin lesion and for some sores in his mouth. So I told him to come to the clinic tomorrow where the pastors can counsel with him after we treat his lesions. They will be able to establish with a lot more certainty what his real living conditions are. It's great to have that kind of support at the clinic. Each day a local pastor is present to talk and pray with the patients and their families.

June 19

So much has happened in the last twenty-four hours, I will simply outline the activity:

Rains came.

Power went off.

Started generator.

Half of house's power went up, half went down.

Pad O'Neil said, "It's happened before." Whew, at least it wasn't all my fault.

Pad finds short circuit (Dave, it's in the bodega somewhere).

Pad fixes problem. Go to Pad's house.

O'Neils' generator won't work (now eight hours into the power outage).

Can't fix their generator. Go home.

No water. I fix the problem this time

Bedtime.

My fever goes up, cough, chest pain. For want of a better term, I call it pneumonia. Antibiotics in the morning.

Restart generator at midnight to save food in the refrigerator. Shut down generator at 1:00 a.m.

Awaken.

Clinic. Today was the day of plugged ears and stomach pains, orphans and live-alones.

No fans. Power still off.

Power finally comes back on after twenty-four hours.

Go home after clinic.

Water off again. Different problem. Fix it (Dave, filter was plugged).

Dinner.

Wow! It's late and dark (nearly 6:30 p.m.). Time for bed.

June 20–21

Each day delivers more excitement than the previous. I just broke the Olympic record for quick treatment of an acute anterior MI. Read on!

Yesterday I was at the house, experiencing the required abdominal queasiness associated with taking antibiotics, when we received a shortwave transmission that we were needed at the clinic. A man was experiencing severe chest pain, which started while he was chasing an errant cow grazing on his property. (There's a history uncommonly obtained at Harborview Medical Center, the hospital where I work in Seattle!) He was at the clinic already hooked up to the EKG machine, but no one knew how to read it. So Matt and I hopped in the Land Cruiser, and, in a fashion reminiscent of scenes from both Jurassic Park and "E.R.," he drove us to the hospital.

WARNING! Medical talk! He had hyper acute ST elevation across the chest leads and had a thready pulse with intermittent vomiting. What medicine did we have? Streptokinase? No. TPA? No. Nitroglycerin? No. Morphine? No. Heparin? No. Lots of no's. Certainly no cath lab, PTCA, or CABG. We did have aspirin. One of the missionaries had four Tylenol #4 tablets at home that he went to get. We found some lidocaine in case we needed it. No defibrillator if we need it, however.

We decided for logistic reasons that we needed to

keep him in the clinic for a while. Don Juan Carranza led the team in impassioned prayer for the patient. They were long-time friends. Nearly everyone working at the clinic and hospital knew him (Don Lencho, Dave; you know him well). About two hours from the onset of the pain, the ST segments were nearly back to baseline. In the States we would have called this a great success for TPA. Here, it was a great success for prayer. He was stable at that point, so we decided to keep him in the clinic overnight. By now we had obtained some other medications from a town about ten miles from here. Nothing fancy, some furosemide, nitroglycerin, atropine. Today he had no ST segment elevation, no chest pain, and no heart failure or arrhythmias. So we drove him home. Now I get to relearn how to do house calls (yes, I'm old enough to remember doing them, though they were infrequent).

June 22

The work team from the States is frustrated. First, there are too few tools, then today, the power was out all day, and they need power tools to do their construction. Improvising, they decided to go swimming in the Caribbean.

Saw my first case of leishmaniasis. It's endemic here, though not too common. We've had a couple of suspected malaria cases, but diagnostic tests won't be back for a few weeks.

June 23

Made a house call to Don Lencho today. As we were approaching his village, we saw him coming toward us on a bicycle (as a passenger). We checked him out, and so far he is doing well.

To church in the evening, where a torrential

downpour made it almost impossible to hear (rain drops the size of golf balls ringing on the tin roof, well almost). But the pantomime done by the gringos was heard just fine.

June 24
The work team went to a local attraction today: the waterfall at Bambu, not to be confused with Bamboo (in the Philippines) or Bantu (in Africa). It cascades downward about seventy-five feet, creating a swimming hole at the base. We stayed there for a couple of hours, no one was anxious to leave because it was sheltered by trees, creating a beautiful oasis.

Tonight the team dines at Chez Maribel (see Honduras, Chapter 3). We hear that the choices again are pollo and pollo. If those don't suit us, there's always pollo.

June 25
Last night we tasted a bit of Balfate culture. The town was having its annual "coronation of the queen," which is sort of like a Miss America pageant. It was held in the town square, and all of the young ladies of the village were decked out in their finest dresses. It was strange to see the fancy silk dresses dragging on the dusty ground as they marched to the rhythm of the local junior high school drum corps. Unfortunately, it began to rain just as they reached the open-air stage platform. We retreated quickly to our house, but most of the town stayed.

Today we attended the Baptist church again, and in the afternoon we paddled a canoe around the local river (like an estuary), sighting many birds that were strange to us—beautiful heron-like creatures and a few red and yellow birds that looked like woodpeckers.

Later in the afternoon, there was a political rally in town for the Honduran presidential election next year. It looked for all purposes like a rally in the States. There were lots of people, food, drink (the wrong kind!), loudspeakers, and speeches. Folks turn out for free food and drink in any country.

June 26
Today's clinic was chaotic! It started with part of the staff arriving late because of a bridge closure just outside of La Ceiba. Some local workers in La Ceiba had declared a strike, which stopped all traffic in town. Two of our staff were coming from La Ceiba early this morning, and they got caught in the strike. Judy studied for about five minutes to obtain her nursing degree and then began the clinic screening.

Then there was a man across the quebrada (ravine) who had a "heart attack." They rushed him to the clinic in Matthew's Ambulance Service, and we quickly determined that he really was having a seizure. He is a binge drinker and has had alcohol-related seizures before. After that, we never quite caught up until the end of the day. A few people had waited without having been assigned an appointment, and we saw them at the end of the afternoon. In addition, the sickest person was the very last one to be seen, and she alone needed about forty-five minutes of attention. It's nice to feel needed.

June 27–28
Tuesday started with more work on the medical laboratory, followed by some strategy planning with Dr. Buddy Dodson, a retired ENT specialist who is planning to move to Honduras, and Jerry Caffey, a contractor who has worked with Cornerstone since its

inception. We walked the property again, looking at the place where Dr. Buddy might build a house. The views were spectacular from the mountaintop.

Clinic was very busy again today. A young girl, age twelve, had a high fever with malaria. There were lots of other people with coughs, sore throats, and stomach pains as well. Dr. Buddy endoscoped a man who had vocal cord polyps. Not ready for surgery yet, just voice rest for three weeks. Lots of hypertension and diabetes here also.

Matt, Dr. Buddy, Jerry Caffey, and Pad did some hiking, looking for a source of water for the hospital and houses that will be built. They found what seems to be a great source of water, about 100 gallons per minute (and this is the dry season!). Matt saw five monkeys and a handful of toucans during the hike. Couldn't help but think of the movie Outbreak because the monkeys were exactly the same size, shape, and color. No Ebola virus here though.

June 29

Ed and Diane Cardwell, a couple from Ohio, were supposed to come to Balfate last night to join us for a few weeks, but they had to cancel their trip. Diane was jogging just before they left and fell, breaking a couple of fingers. She needs some orthopedic work, but they may come later.

Today we harvested some avocados and some "oranges" from the trees in the yard. The avocados are not quite ripe, and the "orange" tree had huge needles on the branches. Not sure exactly what it is, but it's bitter and not like any orange tree I've ever seen. Not that there are many orange groves in Seattle though.

Tomorrow we go to the city, so this tome will get sent.

Preparation for a short-term mission trip can take nearly a year, and you may think that you're ready for anything by the time you finally leave. However, inauspicious beginnings can occur even with the best-prepared teams.

On our trip to the Philippines in 1987, our pastor's wife, Becky, seemed cool, calm, and collected. She had gone through all of the preparations, the cultural training, the drills, and the rehearsals for all expected problems.

But we hadn't prepared her by putting geckos in her bedroom at night. And the room where she slept in the Philippines had geckos on the walls. The first night when she saw them emerging on the walls she screamed, "Steve (her husband and our youth pastor), get these things out of here *now!*" Of course, Steve's reassurance that they would eat insects, which were even more objectionable, did not give her any solace. She just wanted those creatures to leave. After a few hours, she calmed down, but was still not yet a gecko lover. Even the most intense short-term-mission training program cannot prepare a team member for all eventualities. Only by being there are you really there.

Your team must leave itself enough time to prepare for your short-term mission trip. Commonly, in the spring, thoughts turn toward a summer mission trip. This is not nearly enough time to complete your preparations (see Appendix A). Ideally, a member of the team should visit the site a year before the team's departure date. This trip serves many purposes:

- It allows a team leader to see the needs of the recipient ministry.

- It shows the leader how to get to the location (sometimes not an inconsequential task if you must use unfamiliar forms of transportation).
- It makes the leader acutely aware of the living conditions.
- It allows bonding to start between the recipient ministry and the short-term team.
- It shows the leader what arrangements will be necessary for food and lodging.
- It helps the team leader see what supplies might be needed if emergencies arise.
- It reveals additional needs that might not be anticipated.
- It shows the team what equipment might be needed if the project is construction, medical work, etc.

My initial experience in Honduras would have been much easier had someone gone ahead and scouted out what we should expect. While it may seem to be an exorbitant expense to send someone across the ocean for only a few days, the rewards can be immeasurable. If you are bringing a youth team, the parents may be hesitant to allow their offspring to go unless you can describe in detail both the project and the living conditions. Taking a construction team could be worthless if you don't have the proper equipment or if the equipment you take operates on the wrong voltage.

The alternative to traveling ahead of time is to have extremely good communication with the missionary at the destination or to meet with someone who has been there recently and can give you the lay of the land. Our pastor Steve and I took the trip to Guatemala and Honduras mentioned in the previous chapter to see where we should take our youth group. To our assessment, clearly one site was good and one site would have been an abysmal failure, if not dangerous. On-site inspection was invaluable even though we had reasonable mail contact with the missionaries in both places.

Your friends and home church must extensively cover your trip in prayer. For starters, the team must consist only of those persons truly called to go to a foreign land. Not all are called. Some are ordained to witness in Jerusalem or Judea, not in either Samaria or in the uttermost parts of the world. We endeavor to discern the calling of God in each person. Prayer must undergird such discernment. To paraphrase Andy Crouch, a columnist for *Christianity Today*, we must not assume that prayer for our mission trip is simply a request for God to underwrite our dreams.[7]

Prayer is a key component covering the team during preparation, the trip itself, as well as after the trip. We require that all team members have a firm base of prayer support. On our trips, we often require ten families to pray intensively for each member of the team. To remind them of their role, we often supply the folks back home with hospital-style wristbands to wear for the duration of the trip. These wristbands frequently raise opportunities to witness as the supporters go about their stateside activities. The checker in the grocery store asks a man why he is wearing that colored bracelet. A chance to witness. The boss asks a woman if she has been to the emergency room and forgotten to remove the armband. A chance to witness.

The details for the traveling should be planned months in advance. Most airlines have discounts for groups, and prices are always lower if you buy your tickets far in advance. Using a missions travel agent that specializes in planning trips for missions groups can be useful for further cost savings. As someone once said, "Getting there can be half the fun!" One trip to Honduras that I described in

Chapter 3 took six airline flights, one bus trip, riding on a burra (a push-cart on a railroad track), a canoe ride, and a hike. The destination was not really as remote as it sounds, but getting there was a real adventure.

Support and fund-raising must also start as soon as the trip is conceived. It is necessary to have the entire congregation behind your team. Each person going needs encouragement and emotional backing from many people. Involving the congregation from the outset is one way to insure appropriate backing. A note of caution! You must have the wholehearted support of your senior pastor or the congregation will be able to sense any hesitation that may be present. One way to enlist the senior pastor is to have him go on the trip himself (or arrange for him to go on another mission trip). Having the senior pastor go on the "scouting mission" is a useful way for him to learn about the conditions, the needs, and the goals of the mission. Fundraising then is usually not much of a problem. If the church is behind a project, it will happen! We usually require that each team member raise or earn one-third of the expenses himself or herself, one-third is to be raised from donations from close family, and one-third is supplied directly by church funds and special offerings or by projects undertaken by the entire church.

Culture shock (or "entrance wounds," as we call them) is a real phenomenon, especially for anyone who has never left the confines of the United States. As much as you read, and as well as you are coached, you can never be fully prepared for the impact of the foreign environment on your senses and emotions. The language is often different. The activity is intense. The smells are unusual. The food is different. And you're forever on your guard to avoid illness. The customs are strange, and it is difficult to abandon all of the reflexes you've accumulated over your lifetime. You find yourself irritable, angry, confused, depressed, and homesick. But you must still prepare yourself as well as possible for the experience.

Cultural training can be as important as language training. We assume that the North American culture is the norm around the world, but it isn't. Remember that the United States has only 4 percent of the world's population. There's no reason to believe that the rest of the world has the same habits and quirks as North Americans.

Take our notion of time, for example. The clock drives us. If we say we'll meet at noon, it means that everyone is expected to be present about one minute before noon. In other cultures, it's different. If a meeting is planned for noon and the host is having a conversation with a friend, the conversation takes precedence over his timely arrival at the meeting. On the other hand, if you break off a conversation by looking at your watch and saying that you have a meeting across town at noon, the person with whom you're talking is quite likely to be offended. You must study the culture where your team will be serving and adapt to that culture. Though the missionary with whom you will be serving will probably give you a brief orientation when you arrive, you should try to learn as much about the culture as you can before you set foot on foreign soil.

Sensitivity to the people around you is crucial. It is especially important to be sensitive to those who could be offended by your activity, whether it is construction or medical work. In the Philippines in 1987, I had my first experience with medical missions. We had gone to a small village near Bataan and were told that no doctors were available in the area. So we set up a small clinic for a week, and everything seemed to be going well—until the regional healthcare worker arrived on the scene to ask what was going on. He had noticed that very few patients had come to his clinic for a few days, and then he heard that a team was delivering medical care nearby. He was offended that we had not come to him first to discuss our project.

Medical care was very limited in this area, but he was still in charge of the region. Had we gone to him first, we would have had no problems. He would have given his blessing to our efforts. The situation mirrored one of Donald Rumsfeld's rules: "Include others." As Senator Patrick Moynihan (Democrat of N.Y.) said, "Stubborn opposition to proposals often has no other basis than the complaining question, 'Why wasn't I consulted?'"[8] We were quite embarrassed, and we asked his forgiveness for our oversight. We had simply trusted the pastor who had innocently assured us that no doctor was present in his village, and he hadn't mentioned the local healthcare worker. We asked this healthcare worker to come work beside us in our clinic for the next week, and he agreed, reluctantly at first. By the end of the second week, he was a friend and colleague, but our mistake could have been disastrous for the mission trip.

Check your sources. Get the approvals you need. Don't assume that just because you want to work in an under-served area that you can bypass normal channels. This is especially true in medicine but also in other disciplines, such as construction. Obtain the needed building permits, if they are used in the area. Make sure that your street evangelism doesn't block traffic. Don't offend the town by blasting your puppet soundtrack over the loudspeakers at deafening levels.

Personal space is also a cultural concept that must be relearned before you arrive at your destination. The North American has the notion that he "owns" the one or two feet of space around his body. If someone comes closer to us than that, he is "invading our space." We begin to feel very uncomfortable. We fidget. We squirm. But in most other cultures, no such concept exists.

On my first trip to India in 1988, our team was waiting at a train station to buy a ticket (an experience in itself—one line to get an application for a ticket, another line to submit the application, a third line to pay for the ticket, a fourth line to get the ticket, and a fifth line to get a seat). We were clearly the only Westerners in the train station, and we were confused about how to negotiate the process of buying a ticket. At the first window we experienced five or six very friendly Indians crowding around us, chest to elbow, all trying to help but without concern for how tightly our group was packed. Our business was their business. At first, we were concerned that we were being attacked or that someone was going to pick our pockets. But as we looked around, we discovered that such closeness was the norm. Maybe it is because the cities in India are so crowded that they don't give you your space. We discovered as we traveled India for the next three weeks that jostling next to your neighbor on a bus or train was to be expected.

The most common conflict within youth mission teams that we've noted is the issue of a dress code. This issue seems to defy preparation. Clothing in the United States represents a personal expression of freedom. But clothing worn in the United States is not necessarily what other cultures would call modest or even appropriate. We commonly tell our team that shorts are not permitted. Oh, the howls that such a pronouncement elicits! "Why?" "It's not fair!" "What's wrong with it?" "I'm going to wear them anyway!" "Can't we wear them on the construction project?" Let your missionary be your guide for what's appropriate for the culture.

In the Latin culture, for example, even dresses that bare the shoulders are considered to be offensive. Remember that you can preach and sing all you want, but if the people to whom you are ministering have already identified you to be unwholesome or offensive, your witness is ruined. One particularly difficult situation arose in Honduras in 1998 around the issue of women wearing shorts in public. The team leader had finally convinced the women that they needed to be culturally sensitive and not wear shorts in public. Then the missionary's wife showed up at a meeting wearing shorts! Don't think that they had any success with the dress code for that team for the rest of the trip! Some cultures demand head coverings for women, some don't. Become a Roman to minister in Rome!

Sensitivity goes further than avoiding evil. First Thessalonians 5:23 says, "Avoid the appearance of evil." Read it again. It doesn't say, "Don't sin." It says don't even give the *appearance* of sin. We're to strive to remain blameless in the eyes of others, even to the extent that we refuse to do something that may look bad.

When we were in Rwanda in 1994, our leader, Doug Nichols of Action International, frequently had me accompany him on trips around the city of Goma, Zaire. Often my presence seemed useless, and I was unsure why he wanted me to travel with him so frequently. I didn't speak French, the predominant European language of the area, and I knew nothing about the geography of Goma. I had no special expertise in the procurement of supplies, which was why we made these frequent trips.

One day I asked him why he wanted me to go with him on yet another search for rice and beans for our team. He told me that he needed to have Paula, one of our team members, with him because she was the only French speaker in our group, and it was inappropriate for him to travel with her alone. It might *appear* inappropriate to someone, and rumors could start. He needed someone else to go with them. He said that he had learned this principle from the stories he had heard about Billy Graham. To avoid any sense of impropriety, and to keep the name of his ministry above reproach, he would never travel alone by himself with a female co-worker, even on a short car trip down the road. He simply didn't want anyone to have the opportunity to question his morals or intentions. Short-term missionaries must behave no less honorably.

It should be obvious that the short-term mission team must work closely with the local church. All missionaries, whether church planting, doing social service projects, or performing other activities will be affiliated with a local congregation. Most often the missionary will arrange activities for the short-term mission that will support or encourage the local church. However, the team must know what is useful and what is not. The most helpful teams often participate in some service project—building, repairing, cleaning, etc.—as well as ministry, evangelism, or discipleship projects.

I've seen great contrast in what teams call "ministry." The best team I ever saw had planned entire church services, from the opening hymn to the invitation and counseling at the end, in Spanish spoken by the team members. They were amazingly prepared and could conduct a one to two hour service without any assistance, including hymns sung in Spanish with three-part harmony. This team from Michigan worked in Honduras while I was there this year. They had cooperated together as a team on other mission trips for nearly four years.

One and one-half years before the trip, they sent two scouts to Balfate to see what was needed. Then they met every week for an entire year for four to six hours as they rehearsed and re-rehearsed their roles. Each day in their trip was intricately detailed in a playbook that would have made an NFL coach proud. Each church service was scripted to the minute. This is not to say that they were closed to the moving of the Holy Spirit, quite the contrary. But they knew their Plan A well. All church services were done entirely by the team. They did not depend upon any ministry from the local church. Everyone had prepared a testimony and most knew their testimony in Spanish. Furthermore, they planned to do extensive construction work on the hospital and each person had an assigned trade—painting, bricklaying, plumbing, etc. Other teams have done nearly as well, though they have required many translators, which can at times be a burden on the missionaries and the local church.

On the other end of the spectrum was a team I saw last year that requested special services in many churches in the area. Unfortunately, the missionary discovered that all the team had to offer was a short, one-minute skit that was culturally inappropriate. The local pastor was expected to handle the rest of the two-hour service by himself. Clearly a team should have a high benefit-to-burden ratio. It's no help to a local church to add work to their weekly schedule without contributing anything supportive.

Another extreme is the team that wants to do something so complex, and often unneeded, that the missionary must work for weeks or even months to prepare for the arrival of the team. If your building project needs complex structural equipment or supplies, perhaps it would be best to send an advance team of one or two people just to procure the needed materials before the team arrives. An additional note of caution about supplies: developing countries often don't have ready access to many materials, even the simplest kinds. It is quite common to have a team arrive pumped to begin work only to find that the sand and cement are not yet available. Remember the story about Tom spending an entire day looking for a hacksaw blade? Adequate planning for a trip includes advance preparations to obtain the necessary materials for the intended projects.

A team from our church just returned from a mission trip to Chile a couple of weeks ago. It was a group of eleven women who went to support our sister church in El Monte, Chile. An overwhelmingly positive experience, this trip created another eleven people in our church body who are on fire for missions.

They started thinking about the trip in the spring when the Chilean pastor, his wife, and daughter came to our church for our mission week activities. The pastor's wife, Gloria, mentioned that the women in Chile are little appreciated and often ignored. The culture in Chile does not reward them for their tireless efforts on behalf of the church, not that they must be rewarded here on this earth, but knowing they are valuable would be worthwhile. Gloria wanted a team of women to go to El Monte to minister solely to the women—to teach, to encourage, to pamper, to pray with them, and to establish friendships.

The women began to prepare quite late; they started preparing in July for a November trip. They knew they needed more time, but God seemed to be in the project. Their major preparation for the mission trip was not learning the language (three of the eleven already spoke Spanish fluently); not preparing teaching materials (though they did this too); not gathering cloth, knitting needles, crochet thread, and sewing machines (though they did these tasks too); but Bible study and prayer.

They initially met for two hours every Sunday night,

then three, then four. But they always did a complete Bible study first then administrative and preparative activities last. Their priorities were Bible study and prayer. Their goals were *preparation* for the spiritual battle that they knew would emerge, *flexibility* for the certain changes that would confront them both before and during the trip, mutual *submission* to God and to each other, and *humility*. The team was filled with many women who were leaders and administrators, so the possibility for conflict was real, but it never seriously emerged. Mutual submission and the willingness to do any task kept the group unified.

They wisely decided that they needed both an organizational leader and a spiritual leader. One person was not required to do both tasks. The fundraising was a group effort. They felt that God had called them as a team, not as individuals, so all funds received for the trip went into a common fund. Those women who had a lot of friends and contacts who could contribute helped the women who had a smaller circle of supporters, but the solicitation was primarily for prayer support, not for money. Each woman had prayer partners, and each one had a special partner who knew her well and knew her individual strengths and weaknesses. This prayer warrior would know how to pray for this woman—that special prayer was needed for grace to tolerate the rigors of travel, an extra dose of unity, tolerance of the weather, or grace to overcome other weaknesses that might emerge to destroy the mission.

And the trip indeed had its rigors. But upon arrival, their host pastor said, "Remember, you can tolerate anything for two weeks." They knew that their time for these two weeks was not their own but was to be given back to God for His purposes. When they returned, they were asked what they should have done differently that would have improved the experience. Their answer was that they needed to learn more of the language and to understand the customs and cultural norms. They needed to be able to communicate better.

One day Amy, one of the team members, wanted to tell her hostess that her sons were very handsome. She consulted her dictionary, and discovered that the word for "handsome" was *guapo*. She improvised a sentence, but her hostess seemed to react rather coolly. Unfortunately, she later discovered that she had mispronounced it and said *guano*, which means bird droppings. The hostess was initially taken aback, but later they had a good laugh when they finally understood each other. And many other uncomfortable situations emerged that would have benefited from knowing the culture. Is it okay to hug my female hostess? The male host? What clothes are acceptable to wear to church? On a work project? In the host's home? What is the country's concept of personal space? Of hand gestures? Of body language? But the team had a splendid time, and lives—hundreds of them—were changed.

They were often asked by folks back home, "Why not just send the money it would cost for the trip to the church and let them do with it what is most needed?" Our team knew that their own effort would change themselves, influence our church at home, bless the recipient church, and affect both Christian and non-Christian supporters. Money simply sent to Chile could not accomplish all of these goals. And sending money is just too easy. It requires only a small portion of the sacrifice that giving of ourselves does.

Opportunities to witness and to try to break down barriers may appear at quite unexpected times. On my trip to North Korea in 1997, we were continuously bombarded by political propaganda, not to say that visitors to the United States are immune from such harangue. Wherever we went, we heard about the Great Leader or the Son of Great Leader. One day our hosts took us to the border at Panmunjon, and there we were treated to a vigorous dose of rhetoric about how bad the South Koreans were, and, by implication, the North Americans who supported them. At least the North Koreans were polite to us face-to-face.

After an hour diatribe about the South Koreans' faults, we were asked if we had any questions. Initially some of our team members asked historical and logistic questions about how the demilitarized zone operated, but they elicited only the usual political responses. When it came my turn to ask a question, I wanted the tone of the meeting to change, so I asked a question to try to get the North Koreans to alter their thought processes a bit. I prefaced my question with an introduction, "You've probably never thought of this question on your own, and I doubt that you've ever been asked such a question before now,..." hesitatingly, I continued, "but what qualities of the South Koreans and Americans do you most *admire?*"

The North Koreans were visibly distressed. They stammered, never having thought that a long-standing enemy might have any good qualities. Initially they launched into another diatribe about the wickedness of the South Koreans and their governmental policies, but I interrupted them. "No, I understand your differences, but now I want to know what you see in them that you might be able to admire." Dumbfounded, they at least had to think about the question. I don't know what went through their minds, but maybe a small seed was planted. On the last night of our stay in North Korea, we hosted a dinner for our North Korean guides and a few high officials in the Ministry of Health. Up until that time, the pattern for the entire trip had been controlled by our hosts. Everything was done the way they prescribed. We were allowed little or no freedom to address issues that were important to us. But because we were giving the dinner, culturally, they had to allow us to be in charge. We had seen the abject poverty of the country. People were starving under the current government's control and isolation from the rest of the world. Medical care was virtually non-existent. Unemployment was truly a foreign concept. On paper, everyone was employed in North Korea, but in fact, almost everyone was unemployed if you define employment to be gainful or productive activity. We saw no hope for the North Koreans, other than the power of God to begin working on the hearts of the people, perhaps starting with these government officials.

So as we began the evening, we asked them if we could host the meal in a manner familiar to us in the United States. They agreed because it was culturally acceptable for them to defer to us during a meal that we were serving. I asked them if we could begin the meal with a prayer. They knew that they were trapped, but they assented. As I prayed, I asked for God's provision for their country, for healing, for restoration of the ties between them and their neighbors (and in many cases, relatives) in the south. I asked for improvement in their crops, for protection from natural disasters, and for infusion of life back into their medical system. Of course, Dr. Park had to translate all of this into Korean. And if the tears in their eyes meant anything, they understood what I said.

5

"But that's not my job!"

FLEXIBILITY – HOW TO GET THROUGH THE DAY

June 30

Today was go-to-town day. Since we actually accomplished finding a phone to send e-mails, you all should have received the latest installment of my incoherent ramblings. By now you are probably asking yourself, "How can I throttle this guy?" The answer is you can't. You can only ignore me.

Going to town in itself is an adventure. First, there's the drive, which is bumpy and slow but pleasant. Then there's the traffic in town. The Hondurans drive like their tails are on fire and they have no peripheral vision, or fear. I have great apprehension that I might be involved in an accident because the gringo is always at fault. They have a philosophy that any accident would never have occurred if you had simply not come to Honduras in the first place. I guess there's some truth to such an outlook. But no new dents yet! Negotiating the unfamiliar stores is a challenge, but it helps us to improve our Spanish (now was that jabon or jamon?).

One of the hospital workers today was supposed

to drive the army-style truck to town for repairs. On our way to town we passed him only a few minutes out of Balfate. The truck had broken down, but someone had gone to get a part to attempt a repair. As we drove back to Balfate eight hours later, he was still sitting by the side of the road at the same spot, waiting for the part to arrive. Such is life in Honduras. Lots of waiting. Elusive progress.

Matt went with the O'Neils today to San Pedro Sula to get a part for their generator (needed about twice a week, if my sampling is correct). Ten hours of driving to get a part the size of my hand. The store couldn't ship it reliably, so it was necessary to go get it.

At times I feel that my progress here is just as elusive—lots of activity with little forward motion. Many patients walk out of the clinic with the same malady they had when they arrived. We just can't improve their chronic arthritis, stomach pains, or skin rashes. Life has been hard for them. Eighty-five years of swinging a machete. Seventy years of hauling tree branches on the head for firewood. Sixty-two years of walking everywhere you need to go, uphill and down. Today we saw a boy, he couldn't have been seven, working in town "protecting" cars while they were parked. For a small fee, he will insure that no one tampers with your car while you are in the store. What does life hold for him in the next sixty years? Education? No way. Advancement? Where does one go upward from parking lot extortion? Success? Depends on what measuring rod you use. There are thousands like him all over town and in the rural areas as well. There is so little we can do for the thousands, so we must concentrate on the one or two nearby.

July 1–2

Today's sermon was about sweat. No, that's not exactly true. I was thinking about sweat while the pastor was delivering the sermon. Almost the same thing. I was pondering the tireless work being done by the missionaries sitting in front of us. They have been here for six years, since the inception of the idea for the hospital. No telling how many gallons of sweat that they must have donated to the project. Some people keep track of how many pints of blood they have donated in their lives. I think God keeps track of the gallons of sweat expended in His work. These guys have lots of rewards awaiting them in heaven.

July 3

It was 1969. I was an intern at Duke University medical center in North Carolina. A new patient came to the clinic with a fever of 103 degrees. I did a history, physical exam, and embarked upon some lab work. Chest x-ray. Blood count done manually with an antiquated instrument called a hemocytometer. Urinalysis with simple chemicals and a microscope. Diagnosis: pneumonia. Treatment: antibiotics. Admitted to the hospital.

Now it's 2000. I'm working at Loma de Luz hospital in Balfate, Honduras. A new patient comes to the clinic with a fever of 103 degrees. I do a history, physical exam, and embark upon some lab work. No chest x-ray available. Blood count done manually with an antiquated instrument called a hemocytometer. Urinalysis with simple chemicals and a microscope. Diagnosis: pneumonia. Treatment: antibiotics. Can't admit to the hospital because it is still under construction.

The north coast of Honduras is living in pre-1969

medical care, but the living conditions and economy are closer to 1850. When these other conditions improve will the Hondurans health and life expectancy follow?

July 4

Just now I realized that it's the fourth of July. You see, Hondurans don't have a fourth of July. (They skip directly from the third to the fifth.) Hope you guys are enjoying the fireworks. Here we not only have no fireworks but the power was also out for part of the evening (rainstorm).

July 5

Clinic has been a bit more of a challenge these last few sessions. The power company is installing new power lines to the hospital, and they turn off the power from 6:00 a.m. to about 1:00 or 2:00 p.m. so they can work. No fans; no power for things like the computer, etc. But in about six weeks they should have the job completed.

In the clinic today, Judy did the job of nurse, social worker, teacher, lab assistant, pharmacist, patient registrar, translator, cook, errand person, evangelist, and counselor. And that was before lunch.

July 6

Yesterday was a long day. At the end of clinic, one of our clinic workers heard that her brother-in-law was seriously ill in La Ceiba (the commercial radio station actually issued a plea for all relatives to come to see him because he was dying). So we packed the family into the car and drove to La Ceiba. The hospital was amazingly dilapidated. I've seen worse but only in North Korea. Almost no equipment and no supplies. There was only one blood pressure cuff in the entire emergency room, and it was nailed to the wall. He was indeed critically ill, and when we arrived, the other family members were going around town looking for a pharmacy that had the medicines he needed.

You see, they don't supply the medications in the hospital. Whatever you need, the family must find, buy, and bring back to the hospital. Some of the family stayed overnight with him, and the rest of us returned to Balfate. We arrived at 11:00 p.m., which is late in a system where the pattern is to go to bed at 8:00 p.m. and arise at 5:00 a.m. Today we return to La Ceiba to see how he is doing and to bring him some medications from our supply in the clinic.

Today Matt is learning to drive a front-loader and backhoe. He is pushing dirt around at the top of the hill where the water tank will eventually be located. It's a guy thing.

After seeing the conditions in the main hospital in town yesterday, I'm even more convinced that the hospital in Balfate is desperately needed. Pray for its speedy completion.

Since we're going to town, this letter may reach you earlier than it would have otherwise.

Preparation for your mission trip is crucial, but so is flexibility. Paradoxically, flexibility is not the opposite of preparation, as you might expect. In fact, it is complementary to good preparation on the mission field. In order for your trip to be successful, you must be ready to improvise at all times.

Once in 1990 our youth group was preparing to do a puppet show at an elementary school in Guatemala City. Our team was well prepared. All of our youth knew their parts. They had practiced for months. Each person had an assigned character in the script, and we even had substitutes or stand-ins in case someone was unavailable or became ill. Both Dave and Renee could do Chico the puppet. Brad and Adam knew the parts for Enrique. When they arrived at the school, a long drive from our base in the north part of the city, everyone was prepared and excited.

Well, at least excited. Their preparation had not included assigning someone to bring the puppets. The team was at the school. Everyone was present. The sound system was working. The children were there. But no puppets. The team had two alternatives: wait for someone to return to retrieve the puppets (a delay of about 1–2 hours), or come up with Plan B. They chose to improvise Plan B. They divided into teams and organized games for the children to play: soccer, tag, and duck-duck-goose. The children didn't mind. They didn't even know that the program had been entirely changed. The team learned important lessons. Be prepared. Have every aspect of the program covered. Expect the unexpected. Have a Plan B. Listen to the voice of God telling you that Plan B is both needed and allowable.

Most importantly, missions gets the gringo out of his comfort zone. Your comfort zone is that series of routines that is familiar. It's the store where you know how to get a good cut of meat. It's knowing where to go for your oil change. It's being able to say, "I need my oil changed." When you live in a foreign culture, unless you know the language extremely well, everything is a stretch. You don't know how to get much of anything done, and your idea of a project is often very different from the locals' ideas for the same task. But it's only when we attempt the impossible that we see God at work. A good friend once told me, "Don't try to do something that you can accomplish by yourself. That's you working. Try the impossible. Then if it comes to pass you know that you've seen God working."

Often a friend stateside will ask me, "What did you do in Honduras on your trip?" Depending on my mood, I can seem perplexed by this simple question. As I wrote my diary, I would often contemplate, "What did I really accomplish today?" In earthly terms, the answer can often be "Not much!" Simply surviving in a hostile environment can consume every minute of the day.

You try to get an early start, but the power is out and making breakfast becomes a major undertaking. Do you start the generator for electricity? Okay, today you will. But the generator doesn't start. What can you fix that requires no electricity? Then you discover that you have no water either. Ah, but there is propane for the stove. But who wants to heat anything for breakfast when it is already 90 degrees outside? So you settle for bread and jam, sort of like creating a Pop-Tart in the developing world. Then you decide that peanut butter and jelly will do just fine for lunch, thank you very much. But you're now out of bread. No store nearby to get bread, so you settle for crackers and peanut butter. Thank God, the car actually started! So it's off to the hospital. But on the way you meet some folks who need a ride, and the trip is delayed. Then as you arrive at the hospital, you discover that someone needs help over at the bodega (the storehouse). The generator there also needs some work. And the day goes like this until about 9:00 p.m. You discover that the activities of daily living—ADLs as we call them in medicine—have consumed the day. Just surviving took fifteen hours. Maybe tomorrow.

God sometimes delivers hindrances unexpectedly. We may interpret them as problems until we see the larger picture and discover how the problems contributed to the success of a mission. Flexibility, patience, and discernment are needed. In 1991, our YWAM team had finished the three-month classroom phase of the healthcare school in Guatemala City, and the twelve of us were traveling to Honduras for the next three months where we would practice what we had learned. We were carrying with us our small amount of medical equipment and quite a few medications for the patients we would be seeing.

We were going to the interior of Honduras to work with the Pech Indians, who were quite disadvantaged and had no medical care available except for the local *Centro de Salud* (healthcare clinic) that had asked us to come help. We thought that we had covered our bases for crossing the border because we had a letter from the Ministry of Health in Honduras authorizing our entry into the country with our equipment and medications. But it was not to be! The border officials confiscated everything and told us that the Minister of Health was not their boss and that his letter had no force of authority with the border guards. We suspected that they wanted a bribe, but we always refuse to give bribes even if it would seemingly smooth the transaction. (Once you give a bribe, everyone knows that you are willing to participate in this illegal activity, and everyone wants a bribe for everything.)

We were told that we needed to go to Tegucigalpa (the capital city) to get a letter from the customs officials authorizing the import of medications. But Tegucigalpa was a good day's drive from the border, which would mean another day for the return trip. But we had no choice. The border authorities, twirling their revolvers menacingly, were not about to relent. The medications were put in a warehouse for safekeeping (now the new worry that they would be stolen by the time we returned from Tegucigalpa). Then most of the team went on to the interior of Honduras because the local pastor was expecting us, and two team members went to the capital to try to obtain our letter from customs.

The trip itself was an adventure, but surprisingly we were able to see a customs official who gave us the letter and the official seal that we needed. The journey back to the border was punctuated by a few near misses as we drove at night (don't ever do that in a developing country!). The lights on our vehicle were not much more than weak flashlights. Cows were more common than people walking in the road. But the potholes were nearly as big as Chicago, and, more than once, we swerved wildly to miss being consumed by an asphalt abyss.

Upon arriving back at the border, the guards were much more friendly now that we had a letter from their boss, and our prayers that the supplies not be stolen had been answered. We loaded the medications into the truck and began the three-day trip to the Pech Indian village. When we arrived, we discovered that the delay had been a blessing. The team had time to become acquainted with the residents there, and they had even done a community survey of the health status of the village. The villagers trusted them by now, and friendships had already formed. Had the team been able to start clinics on the day of arrival, that bonding might not have taken place and the subsequent evangelism might have been fruitless. As it was, the village leader accepted Christ as Savior, and he wanted to establish a new church in his village that would expose the entire village to the Gospel. The problem at the border was a blessing from God that was difficult for us to see at first. Trust that God is in control and look for His hand in the circumstances.

Your team should also take advantage of unexpected

chances to relax. Relaxation can be difficult for a group that has completing a project as its goal. In 1988, our team was hiking back to Auka, Honduras, after doing a medical outreach in a small village near Tipi. We had hiked into the village a few days before, and we had worked hard doing clinics, church services, and community evangelism for three days. The 100-plus degree heat was taking its toll on us during the three-hour hike home. We reached a small river that we had to cross, and Suzanne, a nurse from North Carolina, lost her footing. The river was only about waist deep, so she was in no danger. Knowing that we would be crossing rivers, we had packed the remaining medications in plastic bags, so nothing in her backpack was ruined. But the sight of someone getting a good drenching was too much for our team to handle. We all threw our backpacks onto the bank and turned the event into a swimming party for a half hour. It was what we needed to break up the monotony of the work, the oppression of the heat, and the gruesome hike. Unplanned, spontaneous fun. Don't leave home without it.

Planned activities for rest and refreshment are also needed. Our church's mission trip two years ago to Chile was a project to build a church in the small village of El Monte near Santaigo, the same village where our women's group ministered this year. The men had only about ten working days, counting a Sunday, both to start and finish the job. They were typical North Americans driven to finish the task at any cost. Every day we received e-mails reporting the progress of the church building. (By the way, e-mail has revolutionized missions. Now it is possible to almost be in constant communication with missionaries and mission teams nearly anywhere in the world. Sometimes the communication is like the messages written at the front of each chapter of this book, sent whenever a person goes to town, but even that intermittent contact keeps the congregation back home informed of the team's progress. Digital photographs can be shown during a church service in the States to depict what's happening in on the mission field.)

It seemed clear that our Chile team could not finish the church construction by the planned departure day. I had been writing words of encouragement to them each day, and with Sunday approaching, I saw that it was tempting for them to forge ahead and ignore God's command for this day of the week. I wrote to them, imploring the team to keep Sunday as a day of rest. They later reported that keeping the Sabbath was a real witness to the Chilean men. In addition, our men were refreshed and believed that their productivity increased so much over the next three days that the building was completed. A double (or triple) blessing.

Often you never know what surprise God has in store for you next. I remember coming home from church one Sunday in Honduras. As we walked the hot, dusty trail back to the bodega (the storehouse we also used as living quarters), a local village child came up to us with a note written on a torn piece of paper. It said, "The ambassador will visit tomorrow."

Now we had absolutely no clue what the note meant. It was 1988, and the Contras were quite active along the Rio Coco, the border two miles south of us between Honduras and Nicaragua. They would foray into the Nicaraguan countryside, and at night many would return to their camps on the Honduran side of the river. Fighting was intense at times, and we could hear the gunfire during the day and at night as we tried to sleep. We were ministering at times to the families of the Contras, though we tried to appear neutral in this most complex of political and military struggles. In our clinics, we treated all men, women, and children if they needed help, but we refused to treat anyone in a military uniform.

So we were sensitized to the struggle going on next door. But a visit from the ambassador? Whose ambassador? And how could that happen out here? The political center of the country was in Tegucigalpa, about a hundred miles away as the crow flies. And if the ambassador was coming here, why tell us with a note on a torn page of notebook paper? Why not some official communication? At least something handwritten on government letterhead. So we dismissed this note as fraudulent at best, a bad joke possibly, or a warning at worst. The concept of a visit from a dignitary was outlandish for many reasons, and so we put it out of our minds.

However, the next day at 10:00 a.m. as we were running a clinic at the edge of the town, we heard the unmistakable chugga-chugga of a helicopter. At first we thought it was just another chopper going to the border with supplies or men for the war. But it kept getting louder and louder. Soon we saw two helicopters come over the horizon. At first it was impossible to tell the nationality of the helicopters because they had been painted solid black. But when the sun hit the side of the choppers just right, you could see "U.S. Army" glistening under the fresh coat of paint. The first landed near our bodega and immediately five or six military men jumped out and ran around our building, brandishing their weapons. We were quickly encircled, obviously out-manned, and quite frightened and perplexed.

At first, we didn't even connect this visitation with yesterday's note. Then the second helicopter landed, and a man and woman emerged from it as though from a movie. They were both dressed in white—immaculate for this part of La Mosquitia. He approached the bodega with long quick strides as though he knew exactly where he was going and what he wanted to do. When he approached us, he introduced himself as the United States Ambassador to Honduras and introduced his wife. They said that they were in the area and decided to drop in. Finally we remembered the perplexing note from the previous day. He apologized that he had not warned us officially but gave no explanation for why the notepaper had been used as official U.S. government stationery.

Quite ill at ease, we managed to offer them a Coke, which they gladly accepted. The visit lasted nearly two hours, as they seemed genuinely interested in knowing why we were there and what we were doing. We seemed a bit like a small United Nations, our team from the United States (Washington, North Carolina, Nebraska, and Texas), Australia, and South Korea. We told them about our mission, which was an unexpected chance to witness to some high-level officials. They expressed gratitude for our efforts on behalf of the poor in the area and then left as quickly as they had arrived. As we reflected on the experience later that night, we were reminded of Paul's admonition to "Be ready always to give an answer to every man that asks you for a reason of the hope that is in you" (1 Peter 3:15).

Yes, the unexpected will greet you on your mission trip. Another humbling episode occurred in the midst of the terrible tragedy in Rwanda in 1994. In the spring, a genocidal massacre began between the two tribes in the area, who had been at war, or at least at odds, for over 400 years. The Tutsis and the Hutus were the two major ethnic groups in the Rwandan countryside, and a series of calamities had triggered one of the worst refugee crises in the history of mankind. The Tutsis had been driven across the country day by day until nearly 2 million persons were fleeing the machetes and clubs of the Hutus.

Millions were fleeing for their lives, and they were forced to run with whatever they could carry on their backs. Politicians, professionals, doctors, lawyers, and engineers, all with their families. Many were quite well educated, but most were ill equipped to live the life of a refugee. They walked, or ran, day after day, week after week, until they reached the border of Zaire (now the Democratic Republic of Congo, formerly the called the Belgian Congo or later just Congo).

Family members frequently became separated, and all suffered terribly as they fled. Those who were not murdered in the flight from their homes often encountered disease, and cholera emerged as a particularly virulent form of illness, at one time killing 10,000 persons per day. Hunger was another foe. With such a large mass of people fleeing, food was either scarce or completely unobtainable. Even when they arrived at the refugee camps set up by the United Nations, the relief agencies could not begin to receive or distribute food quickly enough to prevent starvation.

The details that led me to volunteering to help in the refugee camps were providential. My family and I were vacationing in a small house along the North Carolina shore in July. The refugee crisis had been unfolding for a couple of months, but the magnitude of the crisis was obscure. As we watched the evening news one night, we saw the hordes of people streaming across the border into Goma, Zaire. The inhumanity of the killing and the subsequent exodus was obvious, and we compared the size of the refugee population to the size of the nation of Israel that Moses led from Egypt. As we watched the tragedy unfold over a few nights, my wife turned to me and said, "Someone has to do something." We knew who that someone was, and the next few weeks were devoted to arranging my trip to one of the refugee camps.

I went with a medical team sponsored by Operation Blessing. Our camp was Kibumba, and it contained nearly 350,000 Rwandan refugees. The first few days were spent organizing our clinics and the field hospital. In the process, we met and became instant friends with many of the refugees. Many of them spoke excellent English and some were multilingual. Not the picture I had held of a refugee population from Rwanda.

One day we had a couple of people come up to us and ask if they could help in the clinic. One spoke five languages, the other four. Some groups had managed to remain together throughout the exodus from Rwanda. We worked with one of these groups in our area. The pastor for one group was named Brother John. His entire community had traveled from the far northeast corner of Rwanda to the far southwest corner. Week by week, they were driven mercilessly until they arrived at Kibumba. They set up a small church as one of their first activities, not knowing how long they would be trapped there (it turned out to be nearly a year).

But as we arrived well-fed with our medical team at this center of starvation and cholera, Brother John called us into a meeting in his tent constructed from sticks, grass, and the blue tarpaulins donated by the United Nations. We expected to hear plans for organizing the community, plans to return to Rwanda, or plans for obtaining more food, but we certainly were not prepared to hear what John had to say. Here was an emaciated man, wearied from travel and lack of food, and he shocked us by saying, "Brothers, we must repent, fast, and pray!" Repent, sure. No doubt at least a few of his congregation had participated in some of the atrocities. He knew the hatred that ran between the two ethnic groups. And he knew the proper response before God. Repent, yes. Pray, yes. I can understand that need too.

Here was a man of God who knew the extent of the catastrophe surrounding him. Of course. But fast? Here we Americans came as the embodiment of affluence, and it was our starving brother who entreated us to fast! The unexpected greets us biblically.

6

"Say what?"

COMMUNICATION

July 7

The return trip to the public hospital in La Ceiba was equally as distressing as the first encounter. There were ten patients in a room that would be about the size of two semi-private rooms in a States hospital. No curtains. One very overworked nurse. And it's about as clean as a Jiffy-Lube. Many patients as sick as those in our intensive care unit. Not a doctor in sight. Families holding I.V. bags for lack of I.V. poles. And sadness.

But our friend's relative was much better. He was sitting up, talking, afebrile, eating, and drinking. The wonders of gentamycin and chloramphenicol. Yes, down here they use chloramphenicol without thought for its side effects because it is quite effective and inexpensive. And if an occasional patient dies from aplastic anemia, so be it.

It says in James, "The prayer of a righteous man is powerful and effective." Well, it seems that the quick prayer of a redeemed sinner also works at times. As we were leaving our friend in the hospital, a woman grabbed us and asked if we would pray for her son, who had been in a semi-coma for five days and had not talked for the entire time. They were concerned that he had suffered some permanent brain damage from whatever his infectious disease was (of course, they didn't know his diagnosis). So we huddled with the patient, the mom, and an aunt and said a brief prayer. When we returned a couple of hours later, the woman jumped up and down (really!) when she saw us and hugged us repeatedly. She was praising God for returning her son to her. She said that within minutes of our prayer he awoke and said, "Mom, I'm hungry. Can I have something to eat?" (Sounds amazingly like Mark 5, doesn't it?) Sure, he might have awoken anyway, but the key is that the family gave credit to the Healer and Maker of all creation.

Another day of no electrical power. The power went off at 7:00 a.m. and didn't come back on until 10:00 p.m. We used the generator a bit because the water goes out when the pump can't run.

July 8

Here's a question for you entomologists: What bug represents a cross between a mosquito, a bee, a scorpion, a tick, a gnat, and a chigger?

Answer: I don't know, but it's on my arm now, and forty of them bit me last night.

Actually, they are called sand flies, and they are abundant—you guessed it—along the sandy beaches here. We went walking along the beach yesterday and are paying the price today. The bites itch intensely, and the bumps last for two to three weeks. Fortunately, the disease they may carry is much more prevalent to the east and south of here.

A Saturday night with no power again. We are sitting here by the light of a 12-volt backup bulb, listening to shortwave news from Ecuador. We feel quite disconnected from the rest of the world, which is both good and bad. We don't miss Burger King's, "Have it your way, have it your way," but we do occasionally like to hear what's happening elsewhere.

July 9

Glorious rain, cool rain! A "cold" front came into the area, and the temperature plunged to an overnight low of 74 degrees accompanied by rain and a beautiful lightning storm. What a sight! We had been to the top of the mountain looking for toucans and monkeys (saw none) when the rain arrived.

July 10
MEDICAL TALK ALERT!

Today in the clinic we saw a girl who was nine months old and weighed fourteen pounds. That's not a typo—fourteen pounds! Her mom had walked three hours to get to the clinic, bringing her because of diarrhea, not because of malnutrition. The child was also dehydrated, of course. We discovered that the mom had stopped breastfeeding the child three months ago, and they drank water from the river where the cows and pigs run free. We treated the immediate problem of dehydration and taught her how to purify water with Clorox. When we inquired how much income the family has (a standard part of the clinic questionnaire), she replied, "Nada" (nothing). Some things have no quick and simple solution. We are now trying to discover if there are any malnutrition programs in the area, and, if not, we will try to start one, at least for this one child.

July 11
WARNING! Another medical talk alert!

Alfredo came to the clinic writhing in pain. He is a tough guy who works hard to provide food for his family. No question of secondary gain to this display of anguish. He was in real pain! He had been to another doctor in a nearby village ("nearby," is a relative term) and had been told that he had appendicitis and had to go to La Ceiba for an operation. Never mind that the pain was on his left side, a good example of the reason to build the clinic and hospital in Balfate. (Okay, okay, I know that if he has situs inversus the appendix can be on the left side, but let's talk reality here.) After some tests (Thank God for the recent ability to do urine and blood tests!), we determined that he had a kidney stone. Then the problem was to get the proper medicine. Unfortunately, the narcotics box (yes, we have a few) was locked, and the only person with a key had gone into town and had forgotten to leave the key with us. No problem! (Or, as we say here, "!No problema!") Reinerio, one of the hospital construction workers, displayed an uncanny skill as he quickly dispatched the issue with one strong screwdriver. We didn't ask him if he had ever broken into locked boxes before. Anyone out there want to buy one slightly used and bent narcotics box?

July 12

Matt's Ambulance Service again to the rescue! Someone came to the clinic today reporting that a woman on the other side of Lucinda (a village a few miles away) was suffering severe shortness of breath. Matt had to drive the initial distance on a dirt road then turn right and go up the river. (Don't worry, Dave, the car is okay.) She was having an asthma attack and *was doing poorly when she arrived at the clinic. About four hours later, she was well enough to go home; this time she was driven only to the river, not through the river.*

July 13

Coco is paid an extraordinary salary to be a watchdog at our house here in Honduras. Wasted money! The Drozeks had wanted a guard dog, and Coco applied. She had all of the right credentials. She's a boxer, looks mean, was schooled at the finest guard dog academy, and has sharp teeth. But that's where the resemblance to a real watchdog ends.

Evidence: We had our first real close encounter with "Demon Rum" today. Judy was home alone while I was at the hospital, and Matt was at the O'Neils's. A man who was very drunk came to the front gate of the house, which was unlocked because we had been going in and out a lot today. Coco welcomed him warmly. The man walked up to the front door, accompanied by the hand-licking guard dog, and asked for some food. Coco courageously stood back as the man ate, hoping that some food would fall to the ground. The drunk man then refused to leave. In fact, he became more aggressive and asked for money and tried to come into the house. Coco, adeptly detecting the scent of a human (who, of course, must be a friend), tried to come into the house with him. Judy quickly closed and locked the door, and Coco was quite offended that she couldn't enter the house with her new friend. Judy then called for help on the shortwave radio. The police were called but took two hours to respond, which of course gave Coco adequate time to get really friendly with the intruder. The police escorted the man away, and tonight we can rest assured that we are safe from all intruders, as long as they are not human.

The other excitement for the day was washing the car. Matt and I have decided that we did it all wrong. There is only one way to wash a Land Cruiser. Next time we'll do it the way they do it in television commercials: drive it to the nearest river and look for one large elephant.

We're going to town tomorrow. If cyberspace is working....

Language. It's everything. When it's good, it's great. When it's bad, it can ruin you. Stories about verbal bloopers abound. Unfortunately, most of them are true. Here are a few of them, most of which I personally witnessed:

- A young woman had come from the United States to work in a remote village with a small, emerging church. Her Spanish was marginal, at best. One Sunday in church she was called unexpectedly to the front of the congregation. She was by nature very shy and felt ill-equipped to speak to the group. But she also knew that it was part of her missionary duty to speak to the congregation when asked. She knew that many words in English have equivalents in Spanish with only slight variations in the spelling. So as she stood at the front of the newly constructed thatched building, she launched into a brief description of her feelings. She stumbled into the words to describe her discomfort in being at the front of the congregation. "I'm so embarrassed, and it's all the pastor's fault" for calling her up here, is what she thought she said. Little did she know that the Spanish word "embarrassed" was quite different from the word she used. *Embarazado* means pregnant.

* Our youth pastor's Spanish was limited to a few frequently incorrect words, though he tried diligently. "*Buenos dias, buenas tardes*, and *buenos noches*" were the most common phrases he tried. "Good day or good morning, good afternoon, and good evening" all were combined into a generic "*Buenos noches*," even at breakfast. But he frequently reverted to words he knew from home, and it almost always came out "Buenos nachos." The Mexicans just couldn't understand why Steve was continually complimenting them on their food.

* My wife likes to practice her Spanish everywhere. She also has a limited vocabulary (though not as limited as Pastor Steve's or mine). One day she was talking to some young women in the small town of Balfate. She wanted them to know that her husband (me) had been the love of her life for thirty-two years, but she was a bit uncertain about how to say it. So she simply changed the word "married" to *marido*. Sounded good, and the girls seemed all giggly, so they seemed to get the drift of her story. *Marido* unfortunately means illicit lover.

* Music is often used to cross language and cultural barriers. The tunes and melodies to many hymns and contemporary worship songs are readily recognized in foreign cultures. North Americans are often expected to sing at church services, but it can be a challenge to come up with the words to go along with the tunes. Our youth group loved the song that says, "The greatest thing in all the world is knowing You." Other choruses declare, "The greatest thing in all the world is loving You" and end with, "The greatest thing in all the world is serving You." Never mind the

fact that the song declares three "greatest things," our youth group liked it. They did pretty well through the first two refrains about loving and knowing, but it was the serving verse that got them in trouble. The verb for "serve" is *servirse*. They mispronounced it just a little, and it came out *cerveza,* which means beer. So much for the Guatemalans' respect for our youth.

- On a recent trip to Honduras to help in the relief effort for Hurricane Mitch, our team was blessed with a great person serving as the pharmacist for the medical team. Though an accountant by trade, Russ's attention to numbers and to detail were needed in this position. His Spanish was a bit sketchy, however. Many medication dosages are determined by patient age and size, so he often checked both, like a good pharmacist, when filling out a prescription for a child. *Cuantos años tiene usted?* is literally translated "How many years do you have?" or "How old are you?" He couldn't understand the quizzical look he often received from the children's parents. What he didn't realize was that the "ñ" and "n" in Spanish were said differently and could give a word quite a different meaning. His version of *años* was coming out *anos,* which means anus or rectum. No wonder the parents were perplexed to be asked such a question about their child's anatomy!

- The most recent faux pas was in Honduras last summer when a member of our medical team was instructing a woman how to use the ear drops for her external ear infection. "Put two drops in your ear twice a day" was what Cindy thought she said to Esperanza, the patient, who suddenly looked both dismayed and confused. Esperanza simply shrugged her shoulders and must have thought, "Crazy North

Americans!" *Gotas* in Spanish means drops. Cindy had said *gatos*, which means cats.

You know that you've connected with a culture or a missionary when you begin to think about them after your return to the States. Commonly I will find myself translating what I'm hearing in Seattle into Spanish. I begin to wonder how the Hondurans would respond to the situation I'm witnessing. I have emotional involvement with them even when I'm back home.

The friendliness and camaraderie that accompanies good communication sometimes appear in the most unexpected places. When we were working in Rwanda and Zaire, we frequently had to search for medical equipment and supplies. Each medical organization there became quite familiar with the others, and we bartered almost daily. A bag of rice for a box of intravenous fluids. A case of ampicillin for some surgical instruments. Sometimes we shared ("transferred") patients. ("We'll take some of your patients with dysentery if you'll do the surgery on our man with a gunshot wound.") The French team was the most helpful of all. We understood their language poorly, and they frequently misunderstood us. But even French and English can successfully merge when you have a common goal. Whatever we needed, if they had it, it was ours. And vice versa. Of course, "officially" things like that never happened, but we all knew each other's needs, and we were pursuing the same outcome: keeping the refugees alive and healthy.

One of my early experiences in Honduras taught me about communication and prayer. I had been taken to Auka, a small village in La Mosquitia where communication is essentially non-existent. There were no roads to the region at that time, and everyone who went there had to travel by boat or airplane. After being dropped in Auka by a Mission Aviation Fellowship (MAF) pilot named Steve Robinson, I was acutely aware of my isolation.

One night I was called to see a woman who was in labor in a nearby village. Labor and delivery is not a big deal for an obstetrician, but it's a huge deal for a cardiologist. I clearly was outside of my comfort zone. A few years earlier, the woman had previously delivered a child by Caesarean section, and I was in no position to be able to offer her another C-section. Labor seemed to be going slowly, and I began to wonder if I had any options. When I asked how she had obtained her previous C-section, I was told that the local village leader had gone to the next village and radioed for the MAF pilot to take her to a hospital, which was about forty-five minutes away by airplane. Initially relieved, I asked if we could do the same thing now. The village leader nodded affirmatively but then added that the radio in the next village had not been working for the last year because the battery was dead. Suddenly it added a new dimension to the need for fervent and earnest prayer. God granted us mercy, and the baby was delivered without problems about four hours later, not any too soon for me.

The same setting reminded me of how God must feel when He does not hear from us. I had some difficulty coping with the physical rigors of living in Auka, but my main problem was the isolation, not being able to hear from or talk to my family in the States. As the weeks passed, I wondered what was happening with them. No doubt everything was okay, but one never knows for sure. In the quiet of night, one can fantasize about all kinds of calamities that might befall a wife and four children back home. Did any accidents claim my children? How many broken bones were there? What had gone wrong with the car? Was my wife handling my absence with calmness or with great anxiety? Did our house burn down? Did the dog bite the neighbor? I was not even able to get any global news from the Seattle area of the world. Did an earthquake give us a new coastline? Had rain deserted the Pacific Northwest? Your mind can go on and on. It reminded me that God also wants to hear from us. Of course He knows what is happening, but a prolonged time without communication must also grieve Him. We need to continue daily communication to keep the relationship healthy.

As we have seen before, e-mail has revolutionized communication on the mission front. Now both the short-termer and long-termer can contact supporters and friends almost instantly. Prayer needs that might have taken months to transmit a few decades ago now go out in nanoseconds. This technology adds a new dimension to communication, but it also adds responsibility. Supporters expect to hear from you frequently, before, during, and after the mission trip. Don't disappoint them. Nothing sparks an interest in God's work around the world like being involved in events as they are happening. My journal at the front of each chapter of this book was transmitted every one or two weeks, as often as someone went to town where a phone line existed. When I returned to the States, I discovered hundreds of people who knew about our activities and had been praying for us. I was astounded to see where the letters had been forwarded. Even a nurse in South Vietnam had been reading my scribblings and had been drawn into the emotion of the needs in Honduras.

"God called us to minister here.
He never said we'd come back alive."

PHYSICAL DANGERS, NEEDS AND
CAUTIONS – GOD IS IN CONTROL

July 14–15

We were abducted by aliens. Yes, that's what we'll say. And if we say it with enough fervor, everyone will believe us. It happens all the time. Just watch the X-Files, and you will see something like it for real. We were just sitting in Balfate at noon on Friday minding our own business when this big spaceship came and took us to Tela, another town on the north coast of Honduras. We never intended to go there, but it was imposed upon us. While there for two days, we had to endure the hardships of sitting on the white-sand beaches, playing in the warm Caribbean waters, and eating something other than rice and beans. While we were there, we went to a large national park and bird sanctuary to look for exotic birds. It just so happens that the same spaceship must have abducted all of the birds to Tukwila because we saw none, zero, zilch, or as they say here, nada. We had to go back to the beach to console ourselves. So, really, we didn't enjoy any of it at all! And then Scully and Mulder came in the spaceship and took us back to Balfate. So, you see, it really wasn't a little vacation at all; it was involuntary imprisonment. The fact that we got some rest and worked on a tan was totally incidental. Honest! Now I hope everyone remembers what we're supposed to say!

July 16

Spaceship returned safely to Balfate. Got to get that story straight! Just can't figure out this little computer chip under my skin. And those strange voices that seem to be coming from far, far away.

July 17

Busiest day in the clinic yet. We saw only thirty patients, but some folks were really sick. Hepatitis, congestive heart failure, urinary tract infection, pneumonia, tsutsugamushi (just threw that one in to see if you were paying attention). I would have given my '88 Honda Civic at home for an X-ray machine today, but nobody around here had an X-ray machine to trade. And they would have probably asked for a bit of cash in addition to the car. However, without electricity, it would have been useless anyway. God seems to be impressing upon us that electricity is an overrated commodity. If you actually survive without it, it must not be that important.

The next work team arrived tonight—twenty-two people from Michigan. All twenty-two are learning how to survive without their luggage. Not a single piece arrived with them. Where have we heard that story before? It's like an initiation rite imposed by TACA Airlines to prepare people for the rigors of life in Honduras. The team has one dentist, a nurse, a dental technician, and nineteen people who are good with pick axes and hammers. I just hope they don't get their jobs confused tomorrow morning!

July 18

Another hurricane has hit the northern Honduran coast! It's called the Youth Team from Michigan. Today was their first workday, and they were awesome! They never stopped moving. In fact, we had them hauling some items to a truck to go to the trash dump, and we had to intercept them a couple of times to keep valuable items from being carried out with the trash. It was difficult to find enough jobs for twenty-two people simultaneously for the entire day. And their luggage arrived this afternoon, as though the luggage were saying, "Just testing your resolve, guys. You've passed the first Honduran test. No griping. No complaining. You just rolled with the punches. Way to go!"

July 19

Another record clinic day. Two cardiac consults came from far away, one with echo in hand, a patient with multivalvular rheumatic disease, the other with a VSD. We had to turn away ten to fifteen people, but we screened them quickly to be sure that there were no serious acute illnesses in the bunch. The dentist from Michigan was also kept very busy. She was sad to have to pull teeth that could have been saved in the States.

July 20

Question: Can you have cabin fever if you don't actually live in a cabin and don't really have a fever?
Answer: Definitely yes!
You know that you need a slight change of pace when the prospect of driving to La Ceiba elicits the

emotion of a trip to Disneyland. It is an hour-long trip over a bumpy dirt road through rivers and into a strange place where drivers behave like crazed and hungry cheetahs that have spotted a slow gazelle. Your survival depends upon your reflexes, and your entire life repeatedly flashes in front of your eyes. But the magic was there. It is a real city, we know, because it has paved streets, and we didn't have to compete with cattle for the road. We had a great encounter with a grocery store and a deliriously enjoyable stop at a Pizza Hut. It was Disneyland, considering our state of mind. Did you know that a Pizza Hut menu is actually a piece of fine literature? And that experiencing a choice between orange juice and grapefruit juice is an otherworldly encounter? And, oh, the beauty of the red, yellow, and green of the stoplights! But, by the end of the day, we happily accepted our return to Balfate. We're easily amused, for sure.

July 21

    Emily, one of the Michigan team members came down with cellulitis today—swelling of her leg, hot ankle, and fever. She had experienced some minor trauma to her ankle and an abrasion a few days ago but had been working in the ravine (dirty), on the hospital roof (dirty), in the construction area (dirty), on the bridge (dirty), on the top of the mountain (dirty), and in the grass in front of the staff-housing unit (dirty). See a pattern there? We are quite concerned and even discussed sending her home to Michigan. But we started her on antibiotics tonight, elevated her leg, gave her ibuprofen, and prayed.

July 22

    Emily is better! The swelling is down, the fever is

gone, and there is no more pain. Looks like she may be able to stay here.

July 23

I feel led to write another book. It will be titled Mr. Bug Is Your Friend. *I've outlined a few chapters already:*

Chapter 1: Small Bugs

Chapter 2: Medium-sized Bugs

Chapter 3: Large Bugs

Chapter 4: Bugs That Could Eat a Small Mouse

Chapter 5: Bugs in the Bathroom

Chapter 6: Bugs in the Granola

Chapter 7: Bugs at the Clinic

Chapter 8: Bugs on my Skin

Chapter 9: Bugs That Appear Only at Night

Appendix A: Bugs That Have Caused Judy to Scream

Appendix B: Formula for Calculating When Bugs Will Take Over the World if They Continue to Multiply at Their Current Rate

Appendix C: List of Attempts to Combat the Bug Problem

Appendix D: List of Unsuccessful Methods of Controlling the Bug Problem (same as Appendix C)

Of course, if this book is successful, there are many possible sequels: Mr. Bat Is Your Friend, Mr. Scorpion Learns to Be Nice, Mr. Pig Stops Traffic, *and the* pinnacle of the series, Mr. Sand Fly Has Fun When Leon Is in Town.

July 24

The dental team from Michigan supplemented today's medical clinic. So the chaos was multiplied. The dentists learned to function without electricity;

both the line power and the generator were not working. They worked admirably but could not suppress a loud scream of joy when the power returned at 2:00 p.m.

July 25

We trekked to the top of the mountain today with a couple of the Michigan team members. (It sounds good to say it that way. Paints the picture of a hearty climb, good for the body and soul. Actually, we drove the air-conditioned Land Cruiser.) The view was phenomenal: beach in one direction, mountains in another, and hills with small, thatched huts in another. Toucans, green parrots, rain clouds, and, oh yes, mosquitoes. They don't show them in the Land Cruiser commercials.

July 26
MEDICAL TALK ALERT!

A thirty-five-year-old woman came to clinic today with a six-month history of recurrent syncopal spells, causing her to sometimes fall and hurt herself. On exam she had a slow heart rate of about thirty to forty, cannon A waves, and a mitral regurgitant murmur. The EKG showed a complete heart block with a low, wide ventricular escape rhythm—worthy of admission to a CCU in the States. In Honduras, a pacemaker is a device for the rich. The woman would have to travel to the capitol city to get one and still expect a six-month wait. A tragedy! Her husband is dead, and she has eight children to support. We are trying to get the logistical wheels rolling faster than six months. But even sending her home with any wait seems like a preposterous injustice.

July 27

A fitting place for Judy and me to celebrate our anniversary. Many have been spent in warm climates on the edge of a beach. But here it is with a purpose.

July 28

While we have been here in Balfate, we have learned that many aspects of Honduran life are difficult, such as
heat,
remoteness,
isolation,
diet,
dust,
insects,
transportation,
unusual illnesses,
lack of up-to-date medical information,
no consultations with medical colleagues,
lack of equipment, and
lack of supplies.

But now we are experiencing the most difficult part of all:
leaving.

You will see many things on a mission trip that can be explained and handled only by God. The dangers are real, and the needs are overwhelming. We must never abandon caution, but foremost in our minds must be our belief that God is in control.

I deal with medical issues, while God deals with me. In Mexico City in 1988, the pastor wanted me to examine the mother of one of his church members. She had been sick for a long time, and he wanted our team to visit her in her home and treat her. Upon arrival at the home, we were greeted by a rotten stench that made walking through the front door difficult. In a back room of this small home lay a woman in her sixties who was chronically ill and unable to sit or stand.

When we examined her, we discovered bedsores—decubitus ulcers—so chronic and large that they had totally replaced her buttocks and the upper parts of the backs of her thighs. Even in the United States this condition would have been a two or three year task for an expert team of plastic surgeons, infectious disease specialists, geriatricians, nutritionists, burn therapists, physical therapists, and counselors, not to mention the time needed for routine medical and nursing care. And we were expected to cure her in the five minutes we had been allotted in our schedule of church meetings and evangelistic outreaches. So we had to turn it all over to God in prayer. There was nothing else we could do, yet it was the best we could do. God is in control.

In the Philippines in 1987, we asked a local doctor if there was anything he especially needed. He said that he would think about it and get back to us the next day. When we met the next day, he had a list that included everything from medicines to an ambulance to a new hospital. He had great expectations from the rich North Americans, but we could not deliver. So we had to turn it all over to God in prayer. Again, nothing else we could do, yet it was the best we could do. God is in control.

In Guatemala we were ministering to villagers in the hills, and, as is common, we were asked to go into a hut where a little girl was sick. We encountered a small girl who was about six years old and totally paralyzed from the waist down. Her large brown eyes looked trustingly up toward us, and she had no fear at all of the weird strangers in her midst. She needed many diagnostic tests, but we had none. She needed physical therapy, but we could offer none. She might need surgery, but we could perform none. But she also needed prayer, and we had that available. So we turned it all over to God in prayer. There was nothing else we could do, yet it was the best we could do. God is in control.

In the central highlands of Honduras in 1991, we were making home visits to follow up on patients who had been to the clinic the previous week. As we entered one hut, smoke from the kitchen fire made vision difficult, but we could see a child on a mat on the dirt floor. This child was not the patient we had seen in the clinic. The patient was her grandmother. The grandmother was doing fine with her asthma, though we could see the culprit for the exacerbation of her disease—the smoke in her hut. We immediately turned our attention to the child on the floor. He was lifeless, malnourished, dehydrated, and not breathing, at least the nurse thought so when she first picked up the child. She whispered to me in English, "He's dead!" I quickly examined the child and detected a heartbeat at a rate of about twenty beats per minute and a respiratory rate of about two per minute. Clearly the child was near death. He needed a pediatric intensive care unit, intravenous fluids, intravenous nutrition, perhaps some antibiotics if there was an underlying infection, and about six to twelve months of intensive nutrition therapy to overcome his malnutrition. We had only oral antibiotics. So we had to turn it all over to God in prayer. Nothing else we could do, yet it was the best we could do. God is in control.

On our trip to North Korea, we encountered several hospitals that were essentially closed. Some of them had three hundred bed units but not a single patient, for lack of medicines, equipment, and supplies. The hospitals had no lights, no water or plumbing, and equipment from the 1930s. The country's medical system had received no funding for decades, and it lay in a state of almost irreparable disarray. All the money had gone to the military, to monuments, and to construction projects in the capitol city. Yet the North Koreans thought that these North Americans were going to be able to resurrect their medical system. There were empty medicine boxes on the shelves. We asked the pharmacist why he left empty boxes on the shelves when they contained nothing useful. "For looks," he said. Hope was useful. So we turned it all over to God in prayer. Nothing else we could do, yet it was the best we could do. God is in control.

Your missionary host may need to be coached on the proper approach to handling problems encountered on the trip. One medical clinic in Honduras was particularly busy. It was clear that our team would never be able to treat all of the patients. We prayed that we would be able to do as God would lead, and no doubt it would mean that some patients would not be seen. I decided that I would quietly and prayerfully walk through the crowd to identify the sickest and most needy. However, as I was circulating through the masses of people, the missionary host grabbed a bullhorn and announced, "Dr. Greene is looking for those of you who really need medical care! See him if you want to be treated by a doctor!" I thought that I would be crushed in the stampede! The missionary meant well, but his technique left a bit to be desired. I prayed for guidance to pick the right patients in the crowd and did my best to keep from being mobbed. Nothing else I could do, yet it was the best I could do. God is in control.

One of the reasons I do medical missions, quite frankly, is that people are very appreciative of our efforts, no matter how simple or how apparently futile they may seem. You're paid with hugs and smiles, occasionally with food from their gardens, and once in a while even with items precious to them. One day in Mexico City we were holding a clinic for children, many of whom had serious ear infections. Any mom or dad can tell you how much an earache can distress a small child. Toward the end of the day, I recognized in the line a six-year-old-girl who we had treated the previous day. I assumed that she had waited to get a different treatment because she was still feeling poorly. Maybe the pain was even worse, or maybe she had ruptured her eardrum. But when it came time for her turn, she walked up with her mother and simply said, "*Gracias!*" as she handed me a toy rattle. She was better, had no earache, and wanted to express her gratitude to the gringo who had treated her the day before. As poor as she was, she wanted to give me one of her toys—a small gourd painted to become a colorful rattle. I could see from the look on the mother's eyes that this was a gift I could not refuse. I held it gingerly, knowing how valuable it must be to this little girl. Fourteen years later, I still have it as a reminder of her self-sacrificing appreciation of my feeble efforts to help her in Jesus' name. God is in control.

Regardless of the nature of your mission, you must labor to meet the standards of the country where you're working, and, if possible, to meet the best standards known in the world. Building shabby buildings is a poor witness. Painting a building poorly is a bad witness. Leaving a village with your trash on the ground is a bad witness. Doing medical care poorly is a bad witness. I heard of one ministry that was banned from Honduras because the doctors had rushed into the area, delivered care, and then rushed out a few days later. The authorities discovered that some of the medical personnel had performed procedures for which they were not trained, and a patient had died because he did not receive the appropriate follow-up care. A bad witness.

Our medical team in Rwanda followed another team from the same sending organization, and we assumed that the prior team had investigated the United Nations regulations for hospitals. We did things exactly as our predecessors had done, assuming that procedures were correct. When we were inspected by the United Nations, we were chided for some of our techniques. None of them were serious or dangerous to patients, but they were simply not what the United Nations wanted. We needed better organization. A bad witness.

Sometimes a small dose of spontaneity is appropriate, however. One of my most memorable experiences was a trip to India in 1989 to visit and support a missionary couple in the backwoods country. Our church had supported this couple for nearly ten years, and another couple in our church was about to go to India to work full time in this village with the poorest of the poor in the lowest caste. Jim and I had convinced our wives that we were called to this location, and they both agreed that they did not want to go.

We were an unlikely pair of very Americanized visitors. It was quite early in my short-term mission trip experience, and I didn't really know what to expect. Fortunately we were traveling with Chuck and Joan, our church's frequent short-term missionaries to India, and they knew the ropes. We were planning to fly to Calcutta first, but the four of us were stopped at the check-in counter by a rather nervous ticket agent. He sheepishly told us that our seats had already been given to other people. "Would you mind being separated?" he questioned. "Of course not," we said. Mysteriously, our newly assigned rows had very low numbers, and we soon discovered that we had been bumped to first class. No problem! And Jim and I actually had seats next to each other.

As the trip progressed, I asked Jim an innocent question: "What would you most like to accomplish on the trip?" He was very hesitant and at first refused to answer. Finally he confided, "I really want to meet Mother Teresa!" Well, we had a good laugh at that. Jim had actually been praying that he would get to meet her. He knew that such a request was outlandish, but that was his prayer nonetheless. The Airbus 320 ferried us to our first stop, Calcutta. We quietly discussed Jim's prayer as we descended into one of the poorest cities in the world. I guess I was humoring Jim a bit as I said, "Well maybe God will grant your wish." Little did I know how much our God likes to make us smile! The landing was smooth, and we taxied to the gate; in Calcutta at that time there were no jet ways, just the old-fashioned stairway pushed up to the side of the airplane.

As we watched the stairway come closer, we noted a small contingent of people following the stairs, bunched together as though protecting the person in the center of the group. Since we were in first class, we were one of the first groups to deplane. We finally were able to see this small group better. In the center was Mother Teresa. She had come to meet someone on our plane. No matter whom she had come to greet, we considered it a personal visit to us. Jim was ecstatic, but the protectors kept a tight ring around her so we couldn't get very close. Jim clearly wanted to meet and talk with her, but it seemed like an impossible task. We resigned ourselves to obtaining only a glimpse of her.

As we stood in line to show our passports at the customs and immigration window, Mother Teresa and her entourage went around the security fence and into the airport. It was then that Jim told Chuck about his prayer and his desire to meet her. Well, Chuck stands about six feet, six inches, and he can be an imposing person when he wants to be. He said to Jim and me, "Let's go meet her!" He quickly strode out of the passport line and walked straight up to the guard at the fence separating the incoming passengers from the main part of the airport. "We have an important appointment with Mother Teresa," he said authoritatively. Intimidated by this tall foreigner, the guard opened the gate and let us pass through. We simply walked over to where she was standing with important dignitaries and excused ourselves as we interrupted their conversation.

She was ever the polite, gentle, and comforting hostess as she sat to talk with us, to ask us why we were in India, and to inquire what our missionary friends did in the southern part of the country. Then she invited us to visit the next day her hospice for the sick and dying. After this brief conversation, we returned to the flustered guard and announced, "Thank you. Our audience with Mother Teresa is completed. Now we'll return to the passport line." Jim looked at me and said, "Well, we can go home now. My prayers have been answered, and my goals have been met!" God is so good! And He's always in control.

God does indeed take care of us in the most unexpected ways. In 1991, we were working in Honduras, and it was necessary to rent a car because the team unexpectedly had to split into two groups. The new assignment for our group was to retrieve some equipment and supplies that we had been forced to leave at the border until we had the appropriate papers. The rental car appeared new and seemed to be in good operating condition (emphasis on the word "seemed"). We had to drive through the mountains where the roads are even worse than they are in the flatland.

After we obtained the materials, we drove through the mountains in the Honduran state of Ocotepeque. On the second day, as we were descending a mountain, I applied the brakes only to discover that there weren't any! I had only one option: steer the car into the embankment to stop it. Fortunately we came to a stop before reaching the drop-off where we could have fallen hundreds of feet.

When we opened the hood of the car, we discovered that many of the hoses were old and some of them had been repaired with duct tape. A few even appeared to have been glued together. The outside of the car looked new, but the innards looked like something out of the '60s. We were hundreds of miles from our destination, the team needed our supplies, and our car was terminally ill. Now we had to make a decision.

After considering our options, we decided that we didn't have any. The road was poorly traveled, and it was unlikely that we would meet someone traveling where we were going or had a car in any better shape than ours. So we prayed over the car and began a cautious descent without brakes. First gear to second, second to first, then again and again. We feared that we would wreck either the transmission or ourselves, but we finally made it to the lowlands.

We were feeling somewhat reassured that we were still alive when we stopped at a small gas station in a tiny village. Collectively breathing a sigh of relief, we simply sat for a minute behind the Jeep that was getting gas in front of us. As it started to leave the pump, we suddenly realized that the driver was unaware that we had parked behind her. Before we could retreat or get the presence of mind to honk the horn (if it worked, which it didn't), the four-by-four plowed into the front of our car.

Now our immediate thought was that gringos are *always* responsible for automobile accidents, even though we were parked with the engine turned off. Sure enough, the woman quickly exited her car and blamed us for parking behind her! Her Spanish was rapid-fire, and I was glad we had someone with us who was fluent in Spanish. Nevertheless, it was only minutes before the local police, armed with semi-automatic weapons, of course, were present. Accusations flew through the air, but we finally (and miraculously) convinced one of the policemen that he didn't need to arrest us. Over the next half hour, he even began to agree that the other driver was at fault. Her vehicle was essentially undamaged. Ours, on the other hand, had major front-end wrinkles and crinkles. The right front fender had been pushed back onto the wheel, and the wheel would not turn. The bumper was nearly unrecognizable as a bumper, and, of course, the brakes were still broken.

We managed to find a mechanic in town, which wasn't too much of a problem because by now the whole town was present and looking at the most exciting event to come to the area since a cow ate the Ramirez' family garden about six years ago. This mechanic, by the way, looked like he was about as old as the town itself. He must have been nearly eighty or ninety years old. He surveyed the damage and then proclaimed that he was precisely the man for the job. With a large crowbar, he pried the fender away from the wheel so that we could push the car over to his shop, a corrugated metal roof supported by four poles that looked like they had seen a few earthquakes. Large hammers and crowbars offended our sensibilities, and I could envision the costs mounting. With nothing else to do, I pulled out the rental agreement to find out the limits of my financial responsibility for accidents. The word that came to mind was *todo,* "everything." It seems that the insurance deductible was approximately the value of the car minus one *lempira* (then about 20 cents). No options, though, as *el Viejo* (the old man) continued his banging, pulling, and prying. After about an hour, he declared the bodywork to be finished and asked if we wanted him to look at the brakes. Again, a no-brainer. We had no options. This man had the only car repair shop in this village. There was no judge or federal court nearby to declare his monopolistic activity illegal, so we said, "Sure, go for it!"

Only a few minutes later, he discovered of a leak in the brake-fluid line, and he replaced it with something vaguely resembling a factory-authorized replacement part (looking surprisingly like a small garden hose). After a brief test, he declared his patient cured, and we prepared ourselves for the robbery about to take place. We imagined the bill would be more than the monthly gross national product of the country of Honduras since we were gringos who were obviously rich by the local community standards. Furthermore, we were trapped, and he knew it.

When we asked how much we owed him, he scratched his wizened beard and thoughtfully declared, "*Cinco lempiras.*" Of course, we must have misunderstood him. Five *lempiras* equaled about a dollar, and two hours in a body shop in the United States would have generated a bill of at least $500. Never mind the missing paint, the wrinkles still evident across the front of the car, the tortured look of the bumper; it still would have cost much more in the states. The brake fluid alone would have been more than a dollar at Al's Auto Supply in Seattle. Nevertheless, we thanked him profusely, started the car, and left town quickly before he changed his mind.

But there was still the matter of returning the car to the rental agency in Tegucigalpa. I surveyed the front of the car when we arrived in Tegucigalpa, but I had little experience in auto-body repair. A few years ago in the States, my car was hit by a dump truck that had lost control on an icy hill, and the bill was about $2500. The damage here was similar, so it seemed like it would be about 12,500 *lempiras.* None of us had anywhere near that amount on us or in our bank accounts back home.

I looked again at the rental agreement to see if it mentioned anything about prison terms for destitute offenders. No, nothing. But that's potentially worse—an undefined penalty could be set by *el jefe,* the man in charge. We found the rental agency quickly, much to our dismay because we wanted to avoid the confrontation as long as possible.

I turned the conversation over to the missionary who was fluent in Spanish. I could understand what was being said though. "How was our trip?" "An exciting experience driving through the mountains," he said. "Car work okay?" "Some problems with the brakes," was the reply. Then the moment of truth. "We had an accident. Front of the car damaged." The missionary refrained from saying, "Just take us to jail, and put the key on a freighter to Shanghai." The rental agency employee got his clipboard and walked toward the agency door to look at the car. How is it that a clipboard can look like a ledger book for debtor's prison? He walked around the car, examining the fender-accordion look-alike and the front of the car, which needed some serious ironing. The bumper was still attached, but barely, and the red paint from the other car added a nice touch to our white car. He said "Hummmm" a few too many times as he circled the car twice. "Hummmm" in Spanish apparently means "Hummmm" in English. Images of a cold, damp cell flashed through our minds. How do you say, "Not guilty," in Spanish? Where's divine intervention when you need it?

He wrote with some degree of finality on the clipboard, and then looked directly at us and said, "Looks fixed to me!" There it was! He charged us not a penny for the wreck, though by our standards the car still needed significant repairs. We had even thought—but we restrained ourselves—that we should offer some payment, but he declared that the car was in good enough shape for Honduran streets, and that was the end of the matter. God prevailed and protected us. Add another direct intervention to our tally. God is in control!

Ask me about the worst night in my life, and I'll probably tell you about the night I spent in Puerta Lempira, Honduras, in 1988. We had just returned from a month in Auka in La Mosquitia. At that time, there were only two hotels in Puerta Lempira (well, at least that my friends would tell me about—there could have been some worse ones nearby). The choice seemed obvious—an old hotel that had no plumbing or a new hotel that had indoor plumbing. We chose the indoor plumbing. (My mom didn't raise a fool; I'm just innately stupid!)

Once inside, we inspected the construction and discovered that the windows were at eye level, small, and covered with a rather thick screen. The screen looked good enough to keep the mosquitoes out (remember the name of the region, La Mosquitia). But the plumbing looked suspiciously unfinished. Sure enough, the pipes were there, but the water wasn't. Oh well, we were tired after our trip, and this seemed like a minor inconvenience compared to the past four weeks in the bush. We easily found our room on the second floor, near the only, and non-functioning, bathroom in the entire hotel. The night was unreasonably calm, not a hint of a breeze anywhere.

And though the windows had screens, there were no doors, so the mosquitoes had full run of the building.

By about midnight, I was debating which would be worse: more mosquitoes or the heat. Feeling quite sorry for myself, I began to count the mosquito bites on my legs. I found 200 bites, counting only the anterior portion of one leg. At that point, I abandoned the tally. I decided that a chance of a breeze was worth the risk, just as I discovered that the other two guys in my group were also awake and pondering the same question. So we all climbed onto the roof of the hotel and tried to convince ourselves that we had found a breeze. It probably never dipped below 90 degrees that night, and the mosquitoes had a feast. Worst of all, upon descending back into the hotel room the next morning, we discovered that a thief had stolen our backpacks in our absence. We could only wonder then (and now) what God's purpose for this testing was. But we believed that God is in control!

Food is an idol for some Americans, and it can become the focus of attention on mission trips. I like to think that I eat to live, not that I live to eat. But some mission experiences can teach us how much our gluttony controls us. In my month in Auka, Honduras, in 1988, I had eighty-three meals of rice in a row, including breakfast. The rice left over at the end of the day was, with a little sugar, our breakfast cereal the next morning. We learned how the majority of the world eats every day, month, and year. At the end of our tour of duty there, the local minister had a party for our team and invited a few of the church members. There were twenty-eight of us in all, and I asked our team leader what food would be served for the evening. He replied that the pastor was going to serve us a chicken dish with, of course, rice. My only memory of a chicken over the past month had been one scrawny, tiny animal that we would sometimes see scratching for food along the dusty trail near his house. Sure enough, that night we split one very tiny chicken twenty-eight ways. God is in control!

But my first encounter with dietary issues had occurred years earlier in the Philippines. My mission team was ministering in a remote village with a pastor who lived in the church with his family. There we had existed primarily on rice as well. However, one day my wife looked in the refrigerator (yes, they had one!) and discovered a pig's head in the freezer! Quietly assured that it was only to be used for a special occasion, she forgot about it until the day the team was preparing to go to the beach for a picnic and some relaxation. Early that morning, a large pot had appeared on the stove, and something had been cooking in it for several hours. My wife, being an accomplished cook and wondering what was brewing, lifted the lid and discovered Porky staring back at her. Pig's head is a delicacy in the Philippines, and the pastor had planned to serve it to us at the beach. Suddenly the pork hindquarters, with fat and hairs still attached, that had been served to us earlier in the week seemed like quite an acceptable alternative! (By the way, the other delicacy in the Philippines is *balut*, a nearly-ready-to-hatch chicken that is eaten raw.) These experiences remind me of the mountain climber's explanation for why he does what he does: "It's just like fun, only different."

Some native delicacies are quite good. In Colorado Barra in 1988, our pastor host also gave our team a going-away dinner. On our walk to church on our last Sunday in Honduras, we were met by church members who told us that church had been cancelled. The pastor had gone hunting. It seemed unusual for a pastor, but we accepted the change of plans and had our own church service under the trees, singing and praising God. Later in the day, we were told that the pastor had been successful, and that evening we feasted on a four-foot iguana that he had shot. No, it didn't taste like chicken!

Food can also be a danger. The worst food exposure on the trip in 1988 was also in La Mosquitia. We had taken a canoe to a small village named Srumlaya, where Contra soldiers' families lived, just a few miles from the border of Nicaragua. While we were there holding our medical clinics, I noticed a poor, malnourished little girl pulling a rope through the mud and animal dung of the village streets. She never came to the clinic, so I never saw what she was dragging behind her, but I figured it was a toy. What a pity, I thought, that she seemed to have only this one toy to play with. Two days later, after we had returned from Srumlaya to Auka, we were treated to some meat with our rice. I thought it was actually quite tasty, since we had seen no meat for a few weeks. I made the mistake of asking Andrew what the meat was and where he had obtained it. "Oh, it is deer," he said. "I bought it from a little girl in Srumlaya who was carrying a piece of it around on a rope." But no one became sick. God is in control!

Culinary issues aside, aren't mission trips risky in other ways? Might I get killed in the process? Is it not possible that I could get into trouble with foreign authorities if I venture into an unknown situation? It is said that the first measure of a successful mission trip is the head count on the airplane on the trip home. If you have as many people as you started with, you've been successful.

Indeed, some aspects of a mission trip to a developing country might be treacherous, and tragedies and accidents have happened to short termers. But if you are called to a short-term mission trip, I would contend that it is more risky to ignore God's calling and to stay home than to go to a remote jungle. Once our team came back with one person fewer than it had in the beginning, but for a good reason. The team had gone to Chile to build a building, and a few details were incomplete at the time of the scheduled departure. Jess had been so devoted to the project and to the people we were serving that he chose to stay an extra week to complete the finishing touches. We had a missionary from our home church on-site, so we did not have to leave him alone to fend for himself. It was both a blessing for him as well as the folks in Chile.

Of course, the head count could go up during a trip. It never fails that during our travels we discover some tiny child who needs medical attention or who needs to be adopted. More than once we have come very close to trying to arrange a passport and visa for a child to return with us to the United States, which is obviously a near impossibility.

On one of our church's first mission trips, we had planned to have each member of the team spend an evening with a family in the village to have dinner, to talk, and to learn as much as they could about the culture. We arranged for each team member to go in twos to a church member's home. However, unbeknownst to the pastors, one of the groups of two became a group of one. Even worse, the person was female. She trusted the host and went alone to the home. It was not until three years later that we learned that she had been attacked and assaulted by this person that evening. That is why we absolutely insist that no one ever go anywhere alone, and that women should always have a male escort from our team.

I heard of another team, not ours, that went to Honduras in 1999 with a member who had recently been ill with pancreatitis. He thought that he had recovered sufficiently, though he still had diabetes as an underlying condition. He again developed acute pancreatitis in the jungles of Honduras, and no sophisticated medical care was available. He died before he could get attention. This is why we insist that everyone be in excellent health before a trip. All medical conditions are reviewed with the team leaders. Medications sufficient for the trip are assured. The jungle of the Amazon or a backwoods village in Honduras is no place to discover that one of your team has cancer, or seizures, or a heart condition.

I recall one of my first experiences traveling to a developing country. Again it was 1988, and I was headed to Honduras. In fact, the youth group from my church had just finished a two-week, short-term trip to Mexico, and I was scheduled to continue to travel by myself to Honduras for another month. I was even worse at speaking Spanish then than I am now, and I had a good bit of trepidation about the journey. The trip from Mexico City to Tegucigalpa was uneventful, but upon arrival in Tegucigalpa, I had to clear customs with many suitcases full of medications. Of course, the suitcases contained only medications intended for legitimate use, no narcotics or illicit drugs. But I had the misfortune to describe my cargo as "drugs" (*drugos*), not as "medications" (*medicinas*). In Spanish, there is a big difference. *Drugos* means street drugs, not antibiotics. Immediately I was placed under house arrest, and they confiscated my *drugos* and kept them at the airport.

I was told to return to the airport the next day to confer with the customs chief, who had already gone home for the night. The delay meant that I missed my flight to La Ceiba, my final destination. I was forced to negotiate a taxi ride to the heart of the city and to find a hotel room for the night, a difficult task for an isolated gringo who spoke little Spanish. I spent the night fitfully not only because of the anticipated confrontation the next day but also because I had caught traveler's diarrhea from my previous tenure in Mexico. Nevertheless, I made my way back to the airport the next day, consulting numerous *baños* (bathrooms) along the way. The customs chief was pleasant enough, but I simply could not communicate that these medications were being brought to Honduras for the purpose of helping the poor. He either wanted to confiscate them permanently or charge me a hefty tax for bringing them into the country.

Finally I hit upon a word that made the difference: *Christiano*. I was able to persuade him that I was a Christian and that my goals were humanitarian. He immediately exclaimed, "*Soy Christiano, tambien*" ("I am also a Christian!"). I mentioned the name of the pastor Lamar Costas who was my contact in La Ceiba. He became quite animated and told me that he was a good friend of Reverend Costas' daughter. What a small world! Here I was, a North American with virtually no knowledge of the Spanish language, over a hundred miles from my destination, and we had connected through the pastor's daughter! Afterward, he quickly approved my travel with the cargo of medication (never again to be referred to as *drugos*). Happily, I flew on to La Ceiba on the next flight the following day. When I finally met Lamar Costas, I reported the miraculous story about the customs agent being acquainted with his daughter and how that connection had freed me from hassle, if not danger, in Tegucigalpa. Reverend Costas simply responded with a knowing smile, indicating that he was seeing God at work. "I don't have a daughter," he said. God certainly was in control!

Relief work can become dangerous in some situations. The scene in Rwanda in 1994 consisted of hundreds of thousands of refugees who had been forcefully marched across the country; hundreds of thousands had been killed. Tens of thousands of children were separated from their parents, many of them never to be reunited again. Camp conditions were deplorable—crowded tents, dirty water, cholera, dysentery, and starvation. All conditions that could make rational people become crazed. It was common to have people come to our hospital with gunshot wounds.

Even though all refugees were supposedly members of the same ethnic group, suspicions and innuendo prevailed. Some small groups were suspected of collaborating with the enemy. One morning as we were traveling to the hospital, the driver suddenly warned us, "Look straight ahead! Don't look to the right!" Unfortunately, I was sitting on the right side of the Land Rover and had been photographing some of the street scenes before we left Goma for our camp to the north. I had already seen the man tied to the power pole, head slumped in an unnatural position on his chest and spear-like sticks protruding from his chest. He had suffered the judgment of some local tribunal, and death was his sentence, not to be delayed by the formality of a trial or appeal. It was a sight that will never leave me. Man's inhumanity to man, in the setting of already unconscionable brutality that was claiming hundreds of thousands of lives. One more added to the list. But our team suffered no illness or injury the entire time that we ministered there. God was in control.

Danger can also be self-inflicted. We can do stupid things in a foreign culture. We see the disorganization of some services, such as transportation, and we add to the problem. Guatemala City in 1999, like many large cities in the developing world, was known for its frenetic traffic, and still is today. Cars speed here and there without much regard for speed limits. The concept of traffic lanes seems to have evaded the city planners. Many streets are the equivalent of four- or three-lane roads, but lane markers don't exist. A lane is where you want it to be. Speed is how you define it. Let the driver beware, or the pedestrian. Car-versus-pedestrian accidents are common. One member of our youth team, Charles, almost became a statistic. The team had been working hard on some building projects for many days. It was our first evening to relax, and we had gone to the shopping mall in Guatemala City to eat dinner. The mall there was indistinguishable from a mall in the States—same food, same stores. We parked in a lot across the major thoroughfare from the mall. If one walked to the stop light down the road, the crossing would at least give him an even chance of survival. A few cars actually stop at a red light, and others may slow down a little.

But Charles saw the beacon across the road: Burger King. It was like the voluptuous siren on the shore luring sailing ships to the rocks and sailors to their death. Charles didn't ask; he just bolted across the highway. To be fair, he did look both directions, and he thought he could clear the road before the next wave of cars. Halfway across the thoroughfare, his tennis shoe caught a loose piece of asphalt, and he went tumbling on the pavement. Drivers don't expect, nor do they look for, a crazy gringo rolling on the highway. Charles's only chance to experience the rest of high school was to leap to his feet and continue his run because where he had fallen was beyond the halfway point, the point of no return. Charles was large but fast. He leapt up and dashed to the edge of Mecca, otherwise known as the entrance to hamburger heaven. We came close to returning with one fewer high school student than we had upon leaving. Good thing he survived because the mission trip touched his life permanently. Charles went on to seminary after high school and is now preaching on the mission field. God was in control.

As you plan, you should also think about emergency medical care and even how to evacuate your team, as unusual as it may sound. If you haven't thought about these contingencies, it may be impossible to respond quickly if someone becomes ill or injured. When we went to help the refugee crisis in Rwanda in 1994, we were sponsored by Operation Blessing, a ministry that had a long-term presence in Zaire (now called the Democratic Republic of Congo). They had a number of agricultural projects underway in Zaire, and many Americans were working in villages around this vast country. During part of our orientation (an essential activity), we were told what to do in case political unrest or riots broke out. None of us on the team had remotely considered such a possibility, and it prompted our leader to exclaim, "God called us to minister here. He never said we'd come back alive." But we soon realized that such preparations are reasonable, as witnessed by the fact that two coups have occurred there in the past six years. Operation Blessing had employed two former Navy Seals to plan evacuation details, and we at least knew the basics of what to do in the event of unrest or widespread danger.

A friend told me about an instance a few years ago when the opposite extreme in planning occurred on the north coast of Honduras. A medical team had been working in a small village and had just completed its work there. The team packed up its equipment and began the ride back to San Pedro Sula. Unfortunately, they had adopted the travel habits of the locals. Many team members were riding in the back of an open pickup truck weaving precariously around potholes in the road and traveling at unsafe speeds. As they rounded a bend in the road, they encountered a bus that was taking up most of the road. They careened over an embankment to avoid a head-on collision, and all of the team in the back of the pickup was thrown down the hillside. Many had broken bones, and two were critically injured.

They were unaware of the availability or quality of local medical facilities, and they had no idea where to take the injured for specialized care that they themselves could not provide. They were taken to the nearest local hospital, and it was woefully inadequate to handle their injuries (the reason for the team's presence in the area in the first place). It took over thirty-six hours to discover how to airlift the injured to a stateside hospital, and in the process, two of the team members died. Advanced thought or planning could have hastened the evacuation, and two lives might have been saved. So, as morbid as it may sound, basic inquiries about the local medical care and transport can prevent the long-term effects of illness or injury and may even be life saving. Let God have control.

Visiting mission teams see many needs in their new environment: feeding children at malnutrition clinics, discipleship programs, evangelism outreaches, clothing drives for the naked. Don't, however, assume that your host missionary is blind to these needs. The long-term missionary sees these circumstances day after day, week after week, month after month, and year after year. They are perceptive, or they wouldn't be there long term. They are nearly always stretched to their limit, often unable to handle any new programs. As tempting (or as "God-ordained") as it may seem, don't try to start a program that requires a lot of extra work from the missionary after you leave. You may be able to support the new program by yourself or with the team, but remember the new program will not run itself after you are gone. The long-term missionary may not be able to devote the time that the project needs. Unless it is a program requested by the missionaries themselves, squelch the temptation to start a good work.

Mission trips can also sensitize you to your environment. That's another way of saying that your nerves can be on edge, and it may take very little to rattle you. In Srumlaya in Honduras in 1988, we had set up a medical clinic and were ministering to the families of the combatants in the Contra struggle. We knew that all of the men had rifles, and we could hear the fighting across the border at night. We always wondered why the river kept the fighting on the other side because it was neither deep nor wide. So we were on edge. The end of clinic on the second day was particularly difficult because many more people came than we had resources to treat. Fatigued, we finally made our way back to the hut where we were staying. We collapsed with a good candy bar in hand and were about to drift off into sleep when rapid-fire gunshots erupted just beneath our window.

The shots were close enough for us to smell the gunpowder, bringing us cautiously to our knees, peeking out to see how long it would be before the combatants involved us in this war. Strangely, all of the soldiers were wearing the same clothing, not really uniforms, but the same governmental (or non-governmental, as it were) issue. Then we heard the squeals. Unearthly cries, clearly denoting pain and panic. But these cries were not like any I'd ever heard. Who was being shot? Or, more correctly, what? Wild pigs were scattering throughout the village, creatures that I had only vaguely noticed before this battle. As we peered out the windows, we saw that the soldiers were shooting the pigs without regard for the children playing in the muddy paths or the women walking to the river with their laundry. The families needed food, and they wanted to rid the village of these creatures—two goals accomplished in one barrage of gunfire. I guess the soldiers had such great confidence in their marksmanship that they considered the bystanders to be in no peril from their shots. Just another day in the life of a foreigner to Honduras. Wild pigs. Chaos. Screaming kids. Artillery display. Then the dust settles. Just like Seattle.

"Exit wounds—even when it's over, it's not over"

REVERSE CULTURE SHOCK

August 6
Hi, Gang!
We arrived safely back in the States with no hitches in the return flights. However, here's evidence that we have not yet adjusted to the culture shock of the United States:

1. *I went to a restaurant yesterday (Ivar's, a Seattle landmark that serves mostly salmon), and I wanted rice and beans.*
2. *At work I prepared for an electrical outage from 7:00 a.m. to 3:00 p.m. It didn't happen.*
3. *My diligent attention to avoid cows on the Interstate was unnecessary.*
4. *I was almost arrested today for "second degree excessive friendliness" as I felt compelled to wave at everyone while driving like you do in Balfate. The officer let me off with a stern warning to "just try to be mean next time."*

Have you ever started to tell a joke ("You see, there was this priest, a rabbi, and a pastor ...”), only to realize that you forgot the punch line? It's time for the punch line, and I'm not wise enough to give a fitting conclusion to our mission trip. Perhaps if I respond to the most common questions we receive, it will summarize our experience. The most frequently asked questions are:

1. How was your trip?
2. Did you have fun?
3. What did you do?
4. What did you see?
5. Are you going back?

Usually I respond with short answers because most people don't understand the gravity of their questions:

1. Great!
2. Yes, it was fantastic!
3. Worked in the clinic.
4. Lots of patients.
5. Of course!

But these answers are too glib, too superficial. What I want to say is:

1. It was life changing, both for people in Honduras and for us even though we have gone on a similar trip every year since 1987. It radically alters our outlook on what is important. We have a new view on not letting the tyranny of the urgent divert us from the importance of the eternal. We realized that we lacked a lot of things but none that were essential. We had exactly what we needed when we needed it. We had no excess, but we also had no deficiencies. God supplied things when things were needed, but more often He supplied grace and mercy when they were not.

2. It is hard to describe our experience as "fun."

Looking into the eyes of a malnourished child is not "fun." Watching a man writhe in pain from a renal stone because we don't have any intravenous narcotics is not "fun." Telling an elderly woman that we have no cure for her chronic arthritis is not "fun." And seeing a woman who is passing out because her heart rate is too slow and we can't get her a pacemaker is not "fun." But I believe that the real intent of the question is "Was your trip rewarding?" Yes, it was.

3. *We struggled with our humanness and lost. We turned our weaknesses over to God and succeeded.*

4. *We looked into the eyes of crying children and saw God. We looked into the hearts of elderly Hondurans and saw God. We looked at the needs of the country and saw that God is the answer.*

5. *Our answer to this question is not too revealing. We go somewhere every year, so saying yes really does not speak about the impact of the trip on our lives and our futures. Suffice it to say that we asked the folks there to help build us a small house.*

Thank you for all of your support and prayers. Forgive me for when I have been too verbose.

Serving until His return,
Leon Greene

No doubt that people on short-term mission teams experience culture shock going to a foreign country; everyone expects it. Reverse culture shock can be a bit more perplexing because most people don't know that it will occur, but it will even after a short, one-week mission trip.

One source suggests that re-entry involves four stages:[9]

- Disengagement—moving from the foreign culture back to the United States
- Euphoria—exaggerated happiness at the thought of returning home
- Dampened euphoria—realizing that you have changed, that your friends and family back home do not understand your experience, and that your values have been unalienably altered
- Gradual readjustment—acclimatization and the merging of your past with your recently-acquired mission experience

Here are a few things we have learned upon returning from some of our mission trips:

- Expect to be confused by your emotions—even guy types can have emotions (contrary to what our wives think!)
- Friends and family back home may have "forgotten" about you or even re-aligned friendships as though you don't exist (or even that you "died").
- You will, of course, be saddened to leave the foreign country.
- After a few days here, you may even wonder why you are not ecstatic to be back home.
- You will experience grief at leaving new friends abroad and perhaps even guilt for not having accomplished all of the tasks that were needed (not just the primary project—which may or may not have been completed, but other jobs you could have done if you had more time).
- It will often be difficult for you to verbalize your feelings about these issues. (Yuk! I'm beginning to sound like a psychiatrist!)

- Truly no one will understand:
  - the effort you expended,
  - the work you accomplished,
  - your sacrifice,
  - the poverty you saw, the conditions under which you lived and worked, and
  - your emotions.

On the other hand, you will not fully comprehend what hardships existed at home. Yes, there were probably difficulties and emotions at home that were just as intense as yours. Yet you'll probably concentrate more on your own feelings:

- The U.S.A. will seem to be a strange place to you:

  it's too materialistic;

  it's not spiritual enough;

  the people are narrow without any worldview and many are ignorant of the plight of the rest of the world.

- You may be overwhelmed by the choices that confront you upon return, even as simple as choosing from among the forty breakfast cereals in the grocery store. ("We didn't need them in _____.")
- You will have a new appreciation of real material needs and how we squander resources in the U.S.A. ("Why are they using so much water?" "Why are they wasting food?") And your friends and relatives may not understand such concerns.
- You may note an intolerance in yourself for those who have less mission zeal than you do.
- You may feel a loss of camaraderie with the mission group after being reunited with your family.
- Concentration may be difficult. Your mind wanders back to where you were.

- You may seem preoccupied, distant, or moody to others at home.
- The work at home may seem insignificant compared with the jobs you were doing in the foreign land.
- You will be fatigued (after the adrenalin high wears off) and need time to rest before resuming all of your responsibilities.

These things may seem extreme. Some of your team members will experience many of these emotions, others just a few. Some emotions will be intense, others mild. But everyone needs to understand the process and know what is happening in your minds.

How to cope?
- Acknowledge the issues.
- Talk with family and friends about your feelings.
- Consciously plan to be involved in life back home.
- Stay in touch with the missionaries with whom you worked.
- Seek opportunities to tell others about your trip, individually or in group settings (your home church or home fellowship group is the obvious start).
- Understand that re-adjustment takes time.
- Integrate your experiences and feelings with a plan for the future. Plan on participating in future mission involvement, or integrate the experience with your current employment.

I will never forget my return home from my first "long" short-term mission trip. I was returning from a month in Honduras where I had been isolated from any communication for the entire time. My entry to the States was through the New Orleans airport. My first non-rice food in a month was a wondrous slice of pecan pie in the airport cafeteria. Under other circumstances, I would have rejected it, but it was a luxury. I was so excited to be home, and it was a couple of days earlier than I had planned because one of our group members needed to leave before her visa expired. I called my wife and surprised her. She was especially pleased because it was our anniversary, and she had resigned herself to spending it alone (with our four children, of course). So she was only too glad to drive to the Seattle airport that night to pick me up. But then she wondered if she had picked up the wrong person! Usually quiet and volunteering little information, I talked non-stop for two hours. It confirmed in her mind that missions would play heavily in our future.

The famous twentieth-century philosopher Yogi Berra has been quoted to say, "It's not over until it's over." For the participant in a short-term mission trip, it would be more correct to say, "Even when it's over, it's not over." The re-adjustment to a weird American culture will take time. The memories will persist. And the effect on your life will never disappear.

Summary

"Go ye therefore."
"Who, me?"

TAKING THE NEXT STEP

A wise person once told me, "Don't provide a great summary for anything that you do. Your audience will ignore your lecture or book and simply rely on the summary." So I have mixed feelings about providing a summary, but I'll try.

If this short-term mission manual has any utility, it must impart the following principles:

- *Every Christian* is called to missions. The only issue is *where* you've been called. It may be next door or around the world. Both are valid responses to God's calling.
- The corollary then is that not all Christians are called to foreign missions or even to foreign short-term missions.
- Short-term missions are expensive both in terms of time and finances. The returns are much more valuable, however, than the costs.
- The first step to a short-term mission is prayer.
- The second step to a short-term mission is prayer.
- The third step to a short-term mission is ...(you get the idea).

- Prepare well in advance for the trip itself. Poor preparation insures disaster along the way.
- The key to sanity during the trip is to maintain flexibility. Nothing ever happens exactly as planned.
- Be a servant.
- Understand that you are God's ambassador. In fact, you may be the only representative of God that your host culture ever sees.

As you undertake your short-term mission trip, you will see God at work. Expect to be awe inspired by what He has planned for you! Be prepared to be changed by the experience!

Appendix A

GETTING READY FOR YOUR SHORT-TERM MISSION TRIP

Preparation Timeline for Your Short-Term Mission Trip

Time before Departure	Major Milestones
12–15 months	• Pray about God's leading for your involvement in a short-term mission trip
14 months	• Pastor or mission representative visits potential foreign locations
12–14 months	• Church selects final destination and, if applicable, mission agency • Begin announcements for the trip (in church) • If applicable, turn application into your local church

12 months	• Finalize team roster
	• Approved candidates apply to agency, if using one
	• Team begins to meet weekly, to pray, and to prepare for trip
	• Begin language and cultural training
	• Start planning for service projects, evangelism, etc.
	• Begin intensive communication with missionaries on the field
10 months	• Start writing support letters
	- Outline goals of mission
	- Have team and mission council review letter
	- Generate a list of recipients
8 months	• Apply for passport and/or visa
6 months	• Order airline tickets
	• Begin immunizations
	• Begin collecting materials for work projects
5 months	• Prepare detailed day-to-day schedule
4 months	• Prepare and practice giving testimonies
	• Refine other skills needed for the mission trip (e.g., masonry, plumbing, etc.)

3 months	• If possible, have a weekend retreat with the team to practice service tasks and to bond
1 month	• Pack major items to be taken on trip
2 weeks	• Pack personal supplies
1 week	• Obtain missing personal and team supplies

Principles for Preparing for
Short-Term Ministry

The principles may vary with the project, but here are just a few:

- Pray
  - for wisdom about a calling to a specific people or country,
  - for guidance about a goal or project,
  - for prayer partners to support you before, during, and after the mission,
  - for the provision of finances,
  - for the provision of materials needed for the project,
  - for the time to be released in your schedule for the project,
  - for the preparation of your heart for the ministry, and
  - for the preparation of the hearts of people where you will be ministering.
- Cultivate long-term relationships with the missionaries with whom you'll be working; don't allow the experience to be a one-time-only event.
- Begin to develop a support team months (or years) before you go. You need a large prayer base to cover you on your trip. Fund-raising must also begin months before the trip.
- Learn the language.
- Be flexible.
- Study the culture:
  - Make a conscious effort to work with, and to relate to, the people in the foreign culture; don't just relate to the missionaries and the members of your own group.

- Appropriate dress—You can totally destroy the witness of the team by violating the local dress code. Your clothes should be conservative, functional, and modest. There should be no "why" questions here—follow the leading of your pastors.
- Time orientation.
- Space orientation—Most cultures do not have the North American concept that you own the two feet around you. You may be offended if you do not understand this concept.
- Expression of emotion—A Middle Easterner may seem to be on the verge of strangling his neighbor during a simple discussion about how much sugar to put in the coffee. Gesturing may seem excessive.
- The pace of life will probably be slower in the foreign land; enjoy the delays and use them to build relationships or for fellowship. You cannot make the bus arrive any sooner by grumbling. Demonstrate patience; be ready to stand in line.
- Be sensitive to how the culture values assertiveness versus passivity.
• Be prepared to step out of your comfort zone.
- Savor new sights, smells, and tastes.
- Be ready to rough it.
- Expect little or no privacy.
• Protect your health:
- Obtain all necessary immunizations (requirements vary with the destination country).
- Learn to survive defensively concerning food and drink, rest, and exposure to the elements.
• Leave your "USA knows it all and does it all best" mentality in the States.
• Don't compromise essential principles (construction, medicine, dentistry, etc.) just because you're in a

foreign country; do things the best way possible.
- Be "others" centered.
- When possible, teach your skills to your hosts; it is better for them to know how to weld than to have you do their welding for a couple of weeks.
- Keep a sense of humor.
- Be a servant in all of your actions. Washing dishes may be as much a ministry as preaching.
- Be willing to help with tasks outside of your primary skill area.
- Most ministry is relational. Seek to build long-term relationships; don't just complete a project. The long-term missionary will be there for many years after you leave. Try to be a servant who cultivates these relationships rather than impedes them.
- Don't expect to see immediate results; you may be cultivating ground for another person to reap.
- Don't compare what you see in a foreign country with what you have experienced in the United States.
- Weather is irrelevant.
- Remain positive; God has a plan for you even if you can't see it.
- Your ministry may not be preaching or praying with people for their salvation. It may simply be doing an act of kindness that will prepare them for another witness who will come later. Don't just look for short-term results; go for the long haul!
- Don't bring a tourist or a holiday mentality with you. You are there to serve the Lord.
- Don't make promises or commitments that you cannot keep to fellow team members, to long-term missionaries, or to the locals.
- If you see a job that needs to be done, do it.
- At all times be ready to sing, to pray, to preach, or to die.

What to Expect from a Typical Day

Often a short-term mission candidate will wonder, "What is a typical workday like?" The mission trip should provide no surprises. The workdays (Monday through Saturday) can often be grueling. Here is an example of a typical day on a mission trip:

6:00 a.m.	Arise
6:30	Clean up or shower
7:00	Breakfast (for meals, often part of team cooks while the others clean)
7:30	Devotions
8:30 a.m.–12:00 p.m.	Work projects
12:00–1:00	Lunch
1:00–2:00	Rest (yes, a siesta is needed if in the tropics)
2:00–6:00	Work projects
6:00–7:00	Dinner
7:00–8:00	Rest; travel to ministry location
8:00–10:00	Ministry
10:00–11:00	Clean up
11:00	Sleep

How to Prepare a Testimony

Each person on the mission team should be prepared to give a testimony during the trip (often many times). A testimony is a chance to witness to others. As a witness, you give an account of events that you have seen, events for which you have first-hand experience and that you know are true. Paul said, "Always be prepared to give an answer to everyone who asks you to give the reason for the hope that you have. But do this with gentleness and respect " (1 Peter 3:16), and "Be prepared in season and out of season" (2 Timothy 4:2).

This aspect of the planning can be the most personally revealing for the team members. Many have never thought seriously about the path their lives have taken, and preparing a testimony reveals to them the wondrous works God has accomplished in their lives.

Typically, a testimony is divided into three parts:
• what your life was like before accepting Christ,
• how you accepted Christ, and
• how your life has changed as a result.

The testimony is a chance to tell others about your life, and you are the most qualified person in the world to relate your experience. No one else (except God) knows as much about your journey as you do. Rarely do you have the opportunity to be such an expert on any subject. The goal of a testimony is to tell a compelling story, briefly and concisely. The following principles should help to guide you:
• Above all, be truthful and transparent. Don't embellish the facts. Don't exaggerate.
• Don't be preachy. You can, and probably should, include a favorite Bible verse that has particular

meaning in your life, but don't bash your listeners with too many Scripture references. This is a story about your life and how God has worked in it, not a summary of the books of the Bible.

- Avoid "Christianese" and religious slang. Define all of the words and terms that might be unclear to your listeners.
- Don't assume that your audience knows anything about the Gospel.
- Keep the story brief and to a point. Don't ramble.
- Give all the credit to God.
- Assume that five minutes is the maximum allowable time. You can always expand it if necessary, but it will be hard to shorten if it begins too long.
- Emphasize what God did for you, not what you have done.
- Be specific; don't resort to generalities. It might seem superfluous to you to explain that you received Christ at age eight in an evangelistic tent meeting in Tulsa, Oklahoma, but these details bring life to your story and make it real to the listener.
- Try to make each of the three segments of the testimony follow a theme. (If before accepting Christ your life was lonely, build the story around how it was lonely. If after being saved, it was filled with joy, explain what true joy means to you and how it is manifested in your life.)
- Try to understand your audience. What and how you share will change with who is listening. The six-year-old Sunday school class needs to hear your testimony told in a different way than a group of prison inmates. Try to be relevant and timely for your listeners.
- Pray for guidance for your words and the concepts you'll be sharing.

Deviating from this three-part formula is acceptable. I often give a testimony of what God has done most recently in my life. By reporting what is happening in my life *now*, it brings immediacy to the story. On a trip to the Philippines, I was called upon to give my testimony repeatedly, and I assured the youth pastor in charge of the mission trip that I would never tell the same story twice. Even the passage of one day altered what was happening in my life, and I wanted to relate what God had done most recently for me. (I recall one elderly woman in the first church I attended as a child. She was a dear, sweet woman whom I admired deeply. However, I listened to her testimony over a period of nearly ten years, and it was always the same, word for word, without variation. She never updated the story by adding what God was doing in her life at the present time, and I'm sure that her words would have had more impact on a teenager if she had not dwelt on a remote past that did not seem relevant to me at that time.) Again, try to understand your audience and tell a story that speaks to them in their terms.

How to Write a Support Letter

Each team member should seek support from friends, relatives, and members of their congregation. This letter serves to generate prayer and financial backing for the trip. It should be sent eight to ten months before the trip, if possible, so that supporters can be involved in the planning, as well as the implementation of the project itself.

Information to include in your letter:
- What God has been doing in your life recently
- Goals of the short-term mission
  - Work projects
  - Evangelism
  - Church planting, etc.
- Destination, include the specific city and country
- Who is going
- When the trip will take place and how long it will last
- What is needed
  - Prayer
    > List specific prayer requests and needs
    > Ask your supporters to commit to pray for the duration of the preparation and trip
  - Emotional support—ask your supporters to remember to encourage you as you prepare for the trip
  - Materials—if you have already identified some items needed for the trip (for example, power tools for construction projects, pharmaceuticals for medical projects, books for educational projects, etc.), list these needs in the letter

- Finances
  > Amount needed
  > Time frame
- Personal information—if you have experienced opposition to your going on the trip from friends or relatives, let your supporters know that they need to pray for a change in the hearts of those individuals

Tips for writing the letter:
- Be humble, honest, and vulnerable
- Be yourself
- Be creative
- Be concise
- Share a personal experience about why you decided to go
- Remind the recipient that donations are tax-deductible (if they are)
- Use your own words
- Avoid too many references to yourself
- Check for accuracy, neatness, spelling, and correct grammar
- Have a good friend critically review your letter
- Sign each letter and jot a brief handwritten note on each to personalize it
- Include a prayer reminder card (a small, bookmark-sized card that lists the details of the trip, often with a small photo of you) that the recipient can put somewhere as a reminder to pray for you daily
- Keep the letter to a maximum of one page
- Include a self-addressed, stamped envelope
- Thank your donor/supporter
- Follow up with a phone call

To Whom Should You Send a Support Letter?
- Family members
- Close church acquaintances (don't send a letter to everyone in the church)
- Your church's mission council
- Friends
- Co-workers
- Neighbors
- Utilize lists you already have, such as a Christmas or a wedding list

Be willing to share your plans in church, in home fellowship groups, in Bible studies, in Sunday school, in your home, over coffee, at dinners, etc.

Remember to keep your supporters informed about the progress of your mission by e-mail during the trip, if possible. After you return, you should send another summary letter to your supporters to inform them of the accomplishments of the mission.

Appendix B

CHECKLIST OF THINGS TO TAKE ON A SHORT-TERM MISSION TRIP

Assume that your luggage will not arrive with you. Take a two-day supply of clothes, essential toiletries, all medications, and other crucial items in your carry-on bag. Be aware that some airlines (especially on international flights) will limit you to one carry-on, which includes large handbags, computer carriers, and briefcases. So if you have a briefcase and a carry-on bag or a large handbag and a carry-on bag, you may be forced (and I mean *forced*) to check one of them, and you may never see it again (or at least until your short-term mission trip is completed).

It is wise to have the team bring a supply of essential common medications so that everyone doesn't have to bring a long list of identical supplies. Remember that some medications must be given by a medical professional. The group leader must know each team member's medical history, allergies, sensitivities, and chronic medications.

Your First Aid Kit Should Include:
- Aspirin

- Non-aspirin pain reliever (acetaminophen, ibuprofen, etc.)
- Antidiarrheal (Imodium, Pepto-Bismol, Lomotil, etc.)
- Antibiotics (for treatment of refractory traveler's diarrhea—TMP/SMX, doxycycline, ciprofloxacin, or norfloxacin)
- Antiemetic (Compazine, etc.)
- Antimalarial medication (chloroquin, mefloquin, etc.)
- Anti-allergy medication (Benadryl, etc.)
- Antibiotic ointment
- Antifungal cream (Lamisil, etc.)
- Cough/cold medication (NyQuil, etc.)
- Decongestant (Sudafed, etc.)
- Small bandages, Ace bandages, gauze pads, and rolls of adhesive tape
- Scissors, pocketknife, tweezers, and safety pins
- Thermometer
- Moleskin

Other Important Items to Pack:
- Maps
- Items for the ministry activity (construction supplies, medical equipment, etc.)
- Travel insurance for the group (optional)
- Emergency medical treatment plans
- Evacuation plans

Individuals Should Consider Packing the Following:
- Bible
- Clothing and underwear for one week—It is a good rule to assume that you will be washing your clothes if you are gone for more than one week. Another good rule is "Take half as many clothes

and twice as much money as you think you will need." Be culturally sensitive and adapt to the culture. Even if you do not think a particular style of dress is offensive (shorts on women, for example), you should still dress in accordance with the prevailing mores. Don't fight it just because it's not the "American" way.

- Two pairs of good, comfortable shoes—Adjust your list according to the expected weather (if rain is likely, boots would be good); old tennis shoes or thongs are often useful too.
- Sweater/sweatshirt in case it gets cool in the evening
- Hat (for protection against the sun, wind, water, etc.), raincoat
- Thin, long-sleeved shirt (for protection from the sun and from insects)
- Work gloves
- Money—A credit card can be useful, but remember that many countries have an entrance and/or exit fee that may be as much as $25 to $50 *cash* per person.
- Essential toiletries—On some mission trips, this requirement might include soaps (personal, laundry, and dish detergent) and toilet paper if they are not available at the site.
- Sleeping bag, if needed
- Stuff sack(s)
- Camera, film, extra camera battery—You should be discreet in your use of photography; don't offend your hosts or the people to whom you are ministering.
- Sunscreen
- Chap Stick, hand cream

- Moist towelettes for washing hands when water is unavailable
- Sunglasses
- Bug repellant
- Swiss Army knife or pocketknife
- Medication—Enough for the trip plus a few extra days (in case you get stranded). It is never wise to assume that you will be able to refill your medication in the foreign land. Nevertheless, keep a list of your prescription medications and doses, your allergies, your medical contacts back home, and, if you have a cardiac condition, a copy of your recent electrocardiogram. A copy of your pertinent medical record can also be very useful. Don't forget antimalarial medicine if you are traveling to an area where malaria is endemic.
- Bring eyeglasses, not contact lenses—Have an extra pair of glasses; often prescription sunglasses are needed.
- Pencils/pens, paper, or journal
- Flashlight
- Travel alarm clock/watch
- Foreign language dictionary
- Water bottle (plus tablets, chemicals, or filters for purification)
- Mosquito netting, if mosquitoes are a problem at the destination
- Small radio
- Work tools and supplies for whatever project you will be tackling—Some projects will require extensive lists of tools and supplies (medical trips, construction trips, etc.).
- Small stash of high calorie snacks (for nighttime "munchies" when nothing can be obtained locally)
- Passport, with photocopies of the picture page,

and visa, if needed—Be sure to apply for passport and visa far in advance of the trip. It can take weeks to get these items.

- Copy of all licenses (e.g., M.D., R.N.), diplomas, and certificates
- Pillowcase (stuffing clean clothes in a pillowcase makes a great pillow)
- Bathing suit
- Needle and thread for repairs
- Backpack
- Avoid taking electrical items—If you do, make sure that the electrical requirements (voltage and cycles/second) are the same in the country to which you are going. Electrical adapters are inexpensive and necessary in some places.
- Airline tickets
- Any immunization certificates needed
- Secure passport or money carrier
- A small gift for the host family is a kind gesture, but excessive toys, candies, or gifts for the children in the missionary family or the local village must be discouraged.
- In some circumstances, the host missionary family has major needs that can be met by the arriving mission team. Try to learn the circumstances of the missionaries and attempt to help them however possible.
- Leave your valuables at home. The mission field is no place for gold or diamonds.

Appendix C

PASSPORTS

Passport Procedures

New passport
- Proof of citizenship
- Certified birth certificate (*not* a hospital certificate or an infant baptism certificate)
- Previously issued passport
- Certificate of naturalization
- Two identical passport photos taken in the last six months. It's best to have photos taken at a passport photo establishment. Photos should be
  - 2 in. x 2 in. and
  - on a white or off-white background
- Provide current identification:
  - Driver's license
  - Other acceptable ID
- Completed application form DSP-11
- Pay $60 for a ten-year passport

Passport renewal

- You must have a U.S. passport in your current name issued in the last twelve years and must have been sixteen-years-old or older when the most recent passport was issued.
- You need to submit application form DSP-11.
- Submit most recent passport with application.

For more information, the following web sites are helpful:

- The place to start is www.travel.state.gov/passport_services.html.
- For a listing of places to obtain passports, go to www.iafdb.travel.state.gov/ and enter your state and city.
- To download an application for a new passport, go to www.travel.state.gov/dsp11.pdf.
- To download a renewal application, go to www.travel.state.gov/dsp82.pdf.

Appendix D

FORMING THE MISSION TEAM

Adopting a Code of Conduct

Your team should have its own code of conduct that provides specific guidelines. I have adopted the following as a start:

- When Scripture is clear, follow it! When Scripture doesn't provide specific guidance, avoid the *appearance* of evil.
- Don't cause your brother to stumble.
- Go with an attitude of
  Servitude,
  Ambassadorship,
  Flexibility, and
  Humility.
- Avoid excessive shows of affection, even between married couples.
- There is to be no cohabitation of unmarried persons or sexual relations between unmarried couples.
- Apparel must be modest (judged by the standards of the host culture).

- No smoking, drinking alcohol, or use of other drugs.
- No homosexual activity.
- No gambling.
- Obey all local laws and regulations.
- Strive to provide an effective witness.

Sample Code of Conduct

Before beginning your preparations, it would be a good idea to review this document prepared by Global Connections, a Canadian organization that has attempted to define good practice for a short-term mission.

The Code of Best Practice in Short-Term Mission

Section one — Aims and objectives

1.1 A short-term mission program will have clear aims and objectives. This will include viability and sustainability, and consideration of how the program serves the long-term objectives of the sending organization, the host/partner organization or church, and other interested parties. The program will have a clear place within Christian mission.

1.2 Attention will be given to the benefits to and responsibilities of the participant, the sending organization, the host organization and/or the host local church, and the sending local church.

1.3 Partnership relationships will be established, as far as possible, with host local churches and communities. Attention will be given to ownership and continuity.

1.4 Appropriate sending church involvement will be sought. An agency/participant/church partnership will be developed, as far as is reasonable.

1.5 There will be a commitment to develop the participant through the experience, including giving attention to personal Christian growth.

Section two — Publicity, selection, and orientation

2.1 Publicity materials will be accurate and truthful. They will be targeted appropriately, and used with integrity.

2.2 Publicity will clearly represent the ethos and vision of the sending organization, and will define the purpose of the program in terms of service, discipleship, and vocation.

2.3 The application process, including timescale and financial responsibilities, will be clear and thorough.

2.4 A suitable selection process will be established, including selection criteria and screening. A pastoral element will be included, regardless of the outcome of selection.

2.5 Appropriate local sending church involvement in the selection process will be invited.

2.6 Orientation prior to departure, and/or after arrival, will be given. Team leaders, field supervisors, and field pastoral caretakers, will be briefed.

2.7 Preparatory information (between selection and formal orientation) will be provided as early and as fully as possible.

2.8 Placement decisions will be clear and transparent, will be made with integrity, and will be communicated to all involved (including when changes are made).

Section three — Field management and pastoral care

3.1 Clear task aims and objectives, and where appropriate a job description, will be provided.

3.2 There will be clear lines of authority, supervision, communication, responsibility and accountability. Communication and reporting will be regular.

3.3 Pastoral care and support structures will be established. The respective responsibilities of the sending church, sending organization, host organization/local church, and team leader/job supervisor/line manager/pastoral overseer/mentor will be made clear to all parties.

3.4 Opportunities for personal and spiritual development will be provided.

3.5 Participants will be given guidelines on behavior and relationships.

3.6 With reference to above items 3.1–3.5, culturally-appropriate ways of fulfilling these matters will be sought.

3.7 Procedures covering healthcare and insurance, medical contingencies, security and evacuation, stress management and conflict resolution, misconduct, discipline, and grievances, will be established, communicated, and implemented as appropriate.

Section four — Re-entry support, evaluation, and program development

4.1 Re-entry debriefing and support will be seen as an integral part of the short-term "package" (along with orientation, task supervision, and pastoral care), and communicated as such to participants, field supervision, and the local sending church.

4.2 Re-entry preparation, including placement appraisal, will begin prior to return.

4.3 The agency will have considered its role in assisting the participant through re-entry, including facing unresolved personal issues, and future opportunities and directions in discipleship and service.

4.4 The sending local church will be briefed on re-entry issues and any sending agency responsibilities and expectations.

4.5 An evaluation of agency procedures will be undertaken, including comment by the participant, the sending local church, and any host organization/ local church.

4.6 An evaluation of the responsibilities of the host organization/church (where they exist) will be undertaken. An assessment of whether the host's needs and aims were fulfilled will be carried out. Culturally-appropriate ways of feedback will be sought.

4.7 The results of evaluations will be communicated to relevant managers, for the improvement of future projects.

This code is borrowed from Global Connections and may be found at www.globalconnections.co.uk/code.asp and www.globalconnections.co.uk/code_best.asp. Used by permission.

Prospective Team-Member Application Form

Name:_____

       Last   First   Middle

Home Address:_____

City:_____ State: _____ Zip: _____

Work Address: _____

City:_____ State: _____ Zip: _____

E-mail:_____ Home Phone: _____-_____-_____

Fax: _____-_____-_____ Work Phone: _____-_____-_____

Date of Birth:_____/_____/_____

Parent or Guardian's Name:_____

Address:_____

City:_____ State: _____ Zip: _____

Phone: _____-_____-_____

References (one must be a pastor or elder from your local church):

1) Name: _____

    Address:_____

    City:_____ State: _____ Zip: _____

    Phone: _____-_____-_____

2) Name: _____

   Address:_____

   City:_____ State: _____ Zip: _____

   Phone: _____-_____-_____

3) Name: _____

   Address:_____

   City:_____ State: _____ Zip: _____

   Phone: _____-_____-_____

Prior Short-Term Mission or Third-World Experience:

1) Location: _____

   Duration:_____Year:_____

   Type of Work:_____

   Organization:_____

2) Location: _____

   Duration:_____Year:_____

   Type of Work:_____

   Organization:_____

Passport Number:_____Exp. date:_____

Country:_____Citizenship: _____

Languages Spoken Fluently:

❏ Spanish   ❏ French
❏ Russian   ❏ Portuguese
❏ German   ❏ Italian
❏ Chinese   ❏ Korean
❏ Other:

Specify_____

Signature:_____

Date:_____/_____/_____

Questionnaire for Short-Term Missions Screening Committee

Applicant's
Name:_____

Last   First   Middle

Questions for committee to ask each applicant:

Have you accepted Christ as your Savior?

How is your walk with Christ today?

Why do you think God is calling you to this team? How did He do it?

When was the last time you witnessed to someone locally?

Why do you want to go?

What do you expect to contribute to the team?

What do you expect to gain from this trip?

Are you willing to devote five or six hours per week for the next year to prepare for this trip?

Are you healthy?

Have you ever lived in similar circumstances?

Do you speak a foreign language?

If under eighteen, what do your parents think about this trip? Are they supportive? Would they go along as co-workers and chaperones?

Why should the committee recommend that you be included on this mission?

Medical Work Application Form

Name:_____
        Last   First   Middle

Home Address:_____

City:_____ State: _____ Zip: _____

Work Address: _____

City:_____ State: _____ Zip: _____

E-mail:_____ Home Phone: _____-_____-_____

Fax: _____-_____-_____ Work Phone: _____-_____-_____

Pager Number:_____-_____-_____

Date of Birth:_____/_____/_____

Emergency Contact Information:

Name: _____

Home Address:_____

City:_____ State: _____ Zip: _____

Phone: _____-_____-_____

Professional Information

Profession:
- ❏ Physician   Degree:____ from _____
- ❏ Nurse   Degree:____ from _____
- ❏ Physician's Assistant   Degree:____ from _____
- ❏ Emergency Medical Technician
                             Degree:____ from _____

❏ Paramedic   Degree:____ from _____
❏ Other: Degree:____ from _____

Specify: _____

Medical Specialty, if any:_____

Licensure: Number:_____ State:_____

Non-medical Skills or Special Qualifications:

_____

Church Membership:_____
                              Name of Church

Pastor:_____

Address:_____

City:_____ State:_____ Zip:_____

Phone: _____-_____-_____

References (in addition to the pastor listed above):

1) Name: _____

    Address:_____

    City:_____ State: _____ Zip: _____

    Phone: _____-_____-_____

2) Name: _____

    Address:_____

    City:_____ State: _____ Zip: _____

Phone: _____-_____-_____

3) Name: _____

Address:_____

City:_____ State: _____ Zip: _____

Phone: _____-_____-_____

Prior Missionary, Third-World, or Medical Relief Experience:

1) Location:_____

Duration:_____Year:_____

Type of Work: _____

Organization: _____

2) Location:_____

Duration:_____Year:_____

Type of Work: _____

Organization: _____

Your Health

Physical Limitations?: _____

Medical Conditions:_____

Medications:_____

Allergies:_____

Medical Insurance Carrier:_____

Policy Number:_____

Passport Number:_____ Exp. date:_____

Country:_____ Citizenship: _____

Up-to-date Immunizations:

❏ Diphtheria   ❏ Pertussis
❏ Tetanus   ❏ Meningococcal meningitis
❏ Polio   ❏ Cholera
❏ Typhoid   ❏ Pneumococcal pneumonia
❏ Hepatitis A   ❏ Hepatitis B
❏ Yellow fever   ❏ Measles/mumps/rubella

Languages Spoken   ❏ Spanish   ❏ French
Fluently: ❏ Russian   ❏ Portuguese
                     ❏ German   ❏ Italian
                     ❏ Chinese   ❏ Korean
                     ❏ Other:

                    Specify_____

    Please include a copy of your (1) résumé or curriculum vitae, (2) diploma, (3) photocopy of the photo page of your passport, and (4) medical license with this application.

Signature:_____

Date:_____/_____/_____

Appendix E

How to Stay Healthy

The very fact that a village is the recipient of a missionary or a short-term mission group probably means that the destination is some kind of a hostile environment. Beautiful destination resorts are rarely the focus of missionary activities (though some certainly need to be). The hot and humid, the cold and forbidding, or the remote and wild are the sites for missionary work. So you may need to plan to cultivate some survival skills.

General Information

The technique for avoiding illness on a mission trip can be summarized in a few principles:
- Complete your immunizations.
- Take your preventive medications.
- Always consume clean water.
- Eat only safe foods.
- Be cautious to avoid accidents.

Travel to other countries, especially those in hostile environments, carries certain risks.[10] It is estimated that

20 to 70 percent of all travelers have some health problems,[11] and 1 to 5 percent need to consult medical attention on a trip.[12] Worse, 0.01 to 0.1 percent of travelers will need medical evacuation back to the United States. One person in 100,000 will die on a foreign trip.[13] Infectious diseases are responsible for only 1 to 4 percent of these deaths.[14] Cardiac disease is the most common cause of death, obviously related to long-standing pathology. Unexpected death is most commonly caused by trauma, usually automobile accidents.[15][16] Robberies with assault are also common sources of trauma.

All team members should have a medical evaluation by their own physician at least six months before embarking on the trip. This lead time is necessary in case immunizations are needed that require multiple, spaced injections. It may be necessary to visit a travel or topical medicine clinic because most physicians cannot keep abreast of the many and continuously changing requirements for travel to remote destinations.

You should consult the Centers for Disease Control web site for up-to-date information about your destination, and the team leader should prepare a medical evaluation of all personnel. You should learn what illnesses and emergencies to expect in the members of the team. The jungles of Nicaragua are no place to learn that your pastor has diabetes or a seizure disorder.

Tips on Water Purification

Bottled water is usually safe. (Unfortunately, even some bottled water can be bad. Companies have learned that foreigners will trust and buy any bottled water, so some unscrupulous companies simply bottle contaminated water. However, such experiences are rare.) You should inspect the cap or seal of the bottle to be sure that the bottle has never been opened. Carbonated bottled water is the safest source because carbonation causes the water to be slightly acidic, which can kill some bacteria.

Bottled soft drinks are good but avoid ice. Ice, fountain soft drinks, and freezes may be made with water directly from the tap, which can be dirty. Freezing does not necessarily kill the contaminants in the water. Often your hotel may provide pitchers of water in the room for drinking. Be sure that these pitchers of water come from pure sources and not from the tap down the hall. When in doubt, don't drink it; insist on capped, bottled water. Always brush your teeth with pure water, and wash your hands before eating or preparing food. Coffee and tea are okay if the water has actually been brought to a boil. If in doubt, purify the water.

There are three general classes of water purification: boiling, chemical treatment, and filtration. Boiling is the most reliable purification method. However, boiling is not always practical. (Ever try boiling hundreds of gallons of water for a large group?) The use of iodine, chlorine, bromine, or fluorine will purify your water. Most commercial purification tablets use iodine as the active ingredient, but chlorine is more readily available. Common bleach, which contains a good source of chlorine, can be obtained almost anywhere, and it is quite effective. The more contaminated the water, the more chlorine is needed. Likewise, the colder the water, the longer it will take for the purifying chemical to work. At a minimum, the water should be allowed to sit for twenty minutes after the chemical has been added.

The Centers for Disease Control (CDC) recommend that you use a combination method for purifying water, such as both filtering and chemical (though such a comprehensive approach may not be practical in all situations). Here are the methods:

Boiling: Simply bringing water to a boil is usually adequate. You do not need to boil it for ten or twenty minutes as is commonly believed. However, the dirtier the water, the longer you might want to sustain a rolling boil to purify it. Usually one minute is sufficient. Boiling kills bacteria, viruses, and protozoa. It is a good method, but it has its disadvantages:

- It takes a long time.
- It requires a lot of fuel to purify all of the water you need.
- Water must cool before you use it for most purposes.
- It does not clear the water, so it may still look bad, smell bad, and taste bad.

Filters: Remember that disease-causing organisms are quite small. They are measured in microns. A micron is 1.0 millionth of a meter, or 0.0000394 of an inch:[17]

Parasites	>20 microns
Protozoa	
Giardia	>5–15 microns
Cryptosporidium	>3 microns
Bacteria	>0.2–10 microns
Viruses	>0.004–0.1 microns

Filters that allow passage of 1.0 micron organisms will not protect you against bacteria or viruses. Most commercial filters have a pore size of no greater than 0.4 microns and will remove bacteria, but some allow viruses to pass through. Some commercial filters have an additional iodine resin that help to inactivate viruses. Because much water has large particles that will clog most filters quickly, it is wise to pre-filter water with a paper coffee filter first.

For more details about specific commercial filters, refer to www.travelhealth.com or the REI site (www.rei.com).

Chemical: Adjust doses as noted based upon the likely intensity of contamination. Chemicals will kill bacteria and viruses but will not take care of all protozoa, especially if cysts are present. Chemicals may also leave the water with an unusual taste, color, or smell, and some people, such as pregnant women and people with thyroid conditions, may be harmed by iodine.

Here are some guidelines on using chemicals:

- Chlorine Tablets Halazone—1 tablet (4 mg) per liter, or Potable Aqua, or Globuline
- Iodine Tablets (20 mg tetraglycine hydroperiodine)— 1 tablet per liter
- Liquid Iodine (2% tincture of iodine)—Five drops per liter for clear water, ten drops per liter for turbid water. To remove the bad taste, add fifty mg of vitamin C.
- Liquid household bleach—Five drops per liter of clear water, and let it stand for thirty minutes; or ten drops per liter of turbid water, and let it stand for two hours.
- Powder (calcium hypochlorite (HTH))—Add 1 heaping teaspoon to 8 liters of water, then use 1 ml per 100 ml of water to be disinfected.

Ultraviolet light water purifiers: Some recently developed technology purifies water by irradiating it with ultraviolet light. These devices are cumbersome to carry and use. Furthermore, they require electrical power or solar energy. Their efficacy compared to other techniques is unknown.

Illnesses Commonly Encountered
on Mission Trips

A few precautions are necessary when going on a short-term mission trip. The destination site may have endemic diseases that are unknown or more contained in the United States—tuberculosis, malaria, hepatitis, AIDS, typhoid fever, dengue, leptospirosis, and leishmaniasis, in addition to a variety of parasitic diseases. In many cases, common sense will help protect us from these illnesses. For your benefit, I have compiled a list of the illnesses that most commonly effect travelers to foreign environments along with tips on how to avoid these illnesses.

AIDS

You should assume that HIV infection and AIDS are prevalent wherever you go in the world, but this disease may be more common on the mission field than in your neighborhood at home. Medical missions are the only ones likely to have significant exposure, and medical workers are accustomed to "universal precautions." You should avoid any skin-piercing procedures, such as tattooing, ear or body piercing, acupuncture, or even needles used in medical facilities. Most developing countries do not screen blood products carefully, so transfusions should be avoided (they can also transmit hepatitis). Do not share razors. Avoid elective medical and dental procedures.

ALTITUDE SICKNESS

Ascent to altitude can cause symptoms of dizziness, nausea, lightheadedness, headache, insomnia, shortness of breath, clumsiness, confusion, visual problems, and dry mouth. The symptoms are related to the rapidity of ascent, the absolute altitude, and the altitude of origin. The activity at altitude may cause fatigue.

Prevention is possible by limiting the rate of ascent each day and by limiting physical activity. Medicine such as acetazolamide (Diamox, 125–250 mg twice daily beginning two days before ascent and continuing while at high altitude) can help. More serious forms of altitude sickness can progress to pulmonary edema (water in the lungs) and brain swelling (which can lead to seizures, coma, and death).

BAROTRAUMA

Ear pain is a common malady during airline flights, even with good cabin pressurization. As the plane ascends, the cabin pressure decreases, and the pressure in the middle ear becomes higher than the ambient pressure. Usually this pressure differential simply causes popping in your ears. It is usually not painful because the average person's ear allows equalization of these pressures. However, upon descent, the ambient pressure rises, and the pressure in the middle ear has become lower. It's usually on descent that a problem develops. Because the Eustachian tube connecting the middle ear to the nasal cavity can become compressed by this particular pressure differential and the pressures don't equalize, pain can result. It is actually a relative vacuum in the middle ear that causes the pain. Increasing the pressure in the middle ear, which can be accomplished by holding the nose and forcibly blowing the nose, can relieve it. It can be impossible to get a small child to perform this maneuver, however. If the pressure is not equalized, a ruptured eardrum can result, causing further pain and bleeding.

BITES

Scorpion—The sting of a scorpion can be quite painful, but it is usually not dangerous. The most effective methods for avoiding them are those outlined below for spider bites.

Snake—Snakebites can be painful, but more serious reactions can even be fatal. The type of snakes resident in any part of the world varies greatly. The traveler should ask locals what snakes are present in the region. Avoiding snakebites involves awareness and careful walking. Hiking in the backwoods can be dangerous because snakes may not be visible. Treatment following a snakebite can include making a small incision over the bite and suctioning out the venom with a rubber bulb (not your mouth!). Antivenins may be available locally for the specific type of snakebite encountered.

Spider—Most spiders are harmless. The black widow spider and the brown recluse spider are exceptions. The recluse spider bite may cause skin damage and even ulceration, and the black widow bite can cause muscle spasms and abdominal pain. The best way to avoid these bites is to remain alert to these insects so they can be avoided. Also inspect clothing, hats, and shoes before putting them on, and inspect bedding before retiring.

Tick—The bite of a tick may transmit Rocky Mountain spotted fever, relapsing fever, or lyme disease. You should check your body for ticks frequently after being in fields where ticks might reside.

BLOOD TRANSFUSIONS

It is highly unlikely that a short-term mission worker will need blood transfusions for any reason. Transfusions are only needed for severe, massive blood loss, usually associated with trauma of some kind, though they can be encountered in surgery for other conditions, ruptured blood vessels, or bleeding from the gastrointestinal tract. In most all circumstances, support of circulation can be accomplished with other types of fluid, such as saline. If the needs for a blood transfusion are marginal and you are given the option, by all means refuse any transfusion. The screening and testing of blood in other countries is much more prone to error than it is in the United States. Many diseases can be transmitted by a blood transfusion, including AIDS and hepatitis. It is wise to avoid activities that could result in serious trauma, preventing the need for transfusions in the first place.

CAR ACCIDENTS

The best way to avoid trauma from vehicle accidents is to use the same precautions that you would use in the United States: wear seatbelts, don't speed, don't ride in the back of an open truck, and don't drive after dark in developing countries, especially in rural areas.

CHOLERA

Cholera is usually transmitted through contaminated water. It affects 0.2 persons per 100,000 travelers per month. It causes severe diarrhea, though it can be treated by aggressive fluid replacement. The cholera vaccine is unreliable and not recommended.

DEHYDRATION

Inexperienced travelers are often fearful of the water supply no matter what precautions have been taken. They simply avoid drinking anything and become dehydrated. I often tell my short-term teams that they must use a buddy system, similar to rules for swimming. Your buddy is required to ask you every two hours if you have urinated (not usually a socially acceptable question under other circumstances, but necessary here). If the answer is no, then the buddy must see to it that you drink more water. In addition, a simple question about the color of your urine is useful. Dark orange or dark yellow colors indicate that you are becoming dehydrated. This buddy system is also useful to watch for heat-related illness (see Sun-Related Illnesses).

DENGUE

Dengue fever is a viral disease transmitted by the bite of a mosquito. Mosquitoes carrying dengue more commonly bite during the day and in urban areas. There is no vaccination for it, and there is no specific treatment once a person has the disease. Dengue usually has a five to eight day incubation period. The symptoms are headache, severe eye pain, fever, general malaise, and severe muscle, bone, and joint pain. The bone and joint pain are so severe that the disease is sometimes called "break bone fever." Sometimes vomiting and rash appear.

Avoiding infection can only be accomplished by minimizing exposure to mosquito bites, as outlined in the section dealing with malaria and summarized below.
- Avoid being outdoors at dawn and dusk, the times of maximum mosquito activity.
- Wear long-sleeved shirts and long pants.
- Spray clothing with permethrin to repel insects.
- Sleep under mosquito netting, if possible.
- Don't use any perfumed products.
- Use an effective insect repellant (DEET or other compound).

The following table is a useful summary of other illnesses transmitted by insects:[18]

Insect	Diseases transmitted
Anopheles mosquito	Malaria, filariasis
Culex mosquito	Filariasis, encephalitis

Aedes mosquito	Dengue, yellow fever, filariasis
Mansonia mosquito	Filariasis
Chrysops stable fly	Loa loa
Simulium black fly	Onchocerciasis
Phlebotomus sandfly	Leishmaniasis, sandfly fever, bartonellosis
Tsetse fly	African trypanosomiasis
Tick	Lyme disease, relapsing fever, encephalitis, babesiosis, Rocky Mountain spotted fever
Flea	Bubonic plague, typhus
Louse	Typhus, relapsing fever
Mite	Typhus, scabies
Reduviid bug	American trypanosomiasis

GIARDIASIS

Giardiasis is a parasitic disease that is transmitted through contaminated water. It is characterized by fever, abdominal cramping, gaseous abdominal distension, and diarrhea. It can have an insidious onset, with the symptoms appearing many days or weeks after travel. The treatment is oral metronidazole.

HEPATITIS

The type of hepatitis most likely to be contracted in a foreign country is food-borne and waterborne hepatitis A. Hepatitis A is the vaccine-preventable disease most frequently acquired by travelers. It is prevalent wherever sanitary conditions are poor and where food and water are likely to be contaminated by fecal material. It infects 300 out of 100,000 travelers per month. Its symptoms are fatigue, fever, loss of appetite, flu-like symptoms, nausea, vomiting, itching, jaundice (yellow color to the skin), abdominal pain, or tenderness. Hepatitis B can also cause joint pains and arthritis. Because the illness can affect how the liver handles other medications, the patient should immediately consult with a physician to see if any of his medications should have the dose lowered or discontinued. Adequate immunizations are available for hepatitis A and B, and all travelers should be immunized for these diseases (see Appendix F on Immunizations). Hepatitis A vaccine confers 95 percent immunity after four weeks following the first dose, and it lasts approximately six to twelve months. Two doses provide effective long-term protection.

JET LAG

Symptoms include headache, fatigue, nausea, vomiting, poor appetite, changes in bowel and bladder function, confusion, poor attention and memory retention, difficulty making decisions, poor reflexes, depression, blurred vision, and dizziness. For eastern travel, retire and wake up early for the few days preceding the trip. For western travel, try to stay awake at the destination until night arrives. It takes about one day per hour of time zone change to acclimate to the new time zone.

MALARIA

Many mission trips involve travel to areas of malaria infestation. Malaria is acquired by over 30,000 travelers each year. The highest risk area is sub-Saharan Africa. You should consult the Center for Disease Control website (www.cdc.gov) for information on the type of malaria (if any) likely to be present in your area and the appropriate prophylactic medication. The risk of malaria is worse at low altitudes and during peak mosquito seasons.

Prevention: Chloroquin (Aralen) is often the appropriate protection, though some areas of the world have malaria resistant to chloroquin and other antimalarial prophylaxis is required. For areas where malaria is sensitive to chloroquin, the traveler should take chloroquin as a single dose (500 mg of the salt, or 300 mg chloroquin base) weekly two weeks before travel, every week during the trip, and for six weeks after return from the trip. For travel to areas where the malaria is resistant to chloroquin, there are other options available:

- Mefloquin (Lariam)—250 mg of the salt or 228 mg of the base once weekly two weeks before entering the area and continuing until four weeks after leaving
- Doxycycline—100 mg once daily beginning two days before entering the malaria area and continuing until four weeks after leaving
- Primaquine—30 mg base daily beginning two days before entering the malarial area and continuing until seven days after leaving
- Tafenoquine, a combination tablet of atovaquone and proguanil (Malarone)—one 250–100 mg tablet daily beginning two days before entering the malarial area and continuing until seven days after leaving
- A combination of chloroquin and proguanil (Paludrine)—chloroquin as above, and proguanil 200 mg daily two days before entering the malarial area and continuing four weeks after leaving

Doxycycline and primaquine should not be taken during pregnancy. Doxycycline can cause the skin to be sensitive to sunlight. The side effects of these medications are not trivial. Chloroquin can cause abdominal cramps, diarrhea, ringing in the ears, and dizziness. Prolonged exposure can cause eye problems. Mefloquin has been reported to cause mental problems, convulsions, anxiety, depression, nightmares, sleep disturbances, mental changes, and psychosis. Primaquine can cause blood disorders and anemia. Immediate treatment for malaria, rather than prevention, can be achieved by taking three tablets of Fansidar (a combination of pyrimethamine and sulfadoxine). However, this medication should not be taken by anyone sensitive to sulfa drugs.

An equally important procedure for preventing malaria is to avoid mosquito bites by minimizing exposure to mosquitoes. Here are a few tips to help you lessen your exposure:

- Avoid being outdoors at dawn and dusk; avoid rural areas where malaria is most common.
- Try to stay in air-conditioned buildings—the insects are less active in a cool environment.
- Wear long-sleeved shirts and long pants; avoid dark clothes.
- Sleep under mosquito netting (the netting should cover a large area around you so that you cannot be bitten through the netting).
- Use mosquito coils or candles (e.g., citronella) and aerosol mosquito sprays.
- Don't use perfumed products, scented deodorants, shaving lotions, etc.
- Spray clothing with permethrin to repel insects (do not use this chemical directly on skin). Permethrin can last for weeks when applied properly on clothes, tents, bedding, etc.
- Use an effective insect repellant (such as DEET) on exposed skin (Avon Skin-So-Soft has a minor repellent quality as do products with oil of citronella, but they are not as effective as DEET.)

A 10 percent solution of DEET lasts for about twelve hours; a 20 percent solution for twenty-four hours.

* Many ingested products (B-vitamins, garlic) have been promoted, but their effectiveness is questionable.

Symptoms: Malaria may cause immediate or delayed symptoms. They are often initially misdiagnosed and usually consist of malaise, unexplained fever, flu-like symptoms, sweats, and can include muscle and joint pains. Fevers may follow a pattern of recurrence every two to four days. Often the illness is mild with only recurrent fevers. More serious cases can cause severe headache, destruction of red blood cells causing a dark coffee-colored urine and kidney failure, confusion, brain swelling, coma, and even death. The illness usually appears 10 to 30 days after the mosquito bite, though it can be delayed for up to a year. Even adequately treated cases can recur months or years later.

Treatment: Treatment of malaria, in contrast to traveler's diarrhea, should never be undertaken without medical advice and supervision. It may include chloroquin, primaqine, mefloquin, Fansidar, quinidine, or other medications.

MENINGITIS

Many different forms of meningitis exist, but the most pertinent form for travelers is caused by a certain bacterium called the meningococus bacteria. It can begin abruptly as a high fever, headache, stiff neck, confusion, delirium, and coma, and it can culminate in death. Many cases have a distinctive skin rash early in the illness. Immunization is available and is recommended in endemic areas, especially where crowding is prevalent.

MOTION SICKNESS

Motion sickness most commonly occurs on a boat or an airplane. It is caused by the effect of motion on the inner ear. You can minimize the effects by fixing your gaze on a stationary distant object, such as the horizon. You should avoid most foods and strong smells. Eating only simple foods, such as crackers, may help. Riding in the center of the vehicle can minimize the actual motion encountered. Get fresh air. Prevention can be aided by using medications such as a scopolamine skin patch (Transderm-Scop), Dramamine, Bonine, or Marezine.

PARASITES

Parasites are transmitted in many ways—in food, in water, and by insect bites. The most common parasites are intestinal parasites, which can be avoided by meticulous care while preparing food and treating water. Washing hands frequently is a must. Always wear shoes (some parasites can enter through the skin of the soles of the feet). Cooking food thoroughly goes a long way toward preventing parasitic infestation. Many parasites do not cause symptoms until days or weeks after the trip, so be sure to tell your doctor where you have traveled if you become sick after returning home. In fact, it may be useful to give each team member a list of potential exposures to have with them after return to the States so that they can give this list to a doctor (As an example, following this section is a list I made to give to a group that recently worked with me in Honduras.)

RABIES

A traveler may experience an animal bite at a rate of 1 to 2 percent per year in developing countries.[19] You should avoid petting or feeding stray animals. Be especially careful around animals that appear sick. Remember that a sick wild animal may appear tame. It may be difficult to obtain treatment after a bite in a developing country, so if a person is planning to reside for more than six months in a developing country where rabies is endemic (especially Thailand, Philippines, India, Central and West Africa, and Latin America), it is wise to obtain vaccinations prior to the trip, requiring three doses over one month. Following any contact of an animal's saliva with broken skin, wash the area thoroughly with soap, and then use alcohol or iodine to cleanse the wound. You should then seek medical attention for further care because even a person who received three doses of pre-exposure vaccine needs an additional two post-exposure doses.

RESPIRATORY INFECTIONS

Upper respiratory infections are the second most common form of illness on mission trips. Travelers reside in close quarters and are exposed to many persons—conditions that are quite conducive to transmitting respiratory diseases. These infections are most always viral, self-limited, and minor, though disruptive for all concerned.

SUN-RELATED ILLNESS

Dehydration may accompany any of the following heat-related symptoms, so adequate fluid replenishment is always necessary. You should always wear light-colored, thin, and loose-fitting clothing.

Heat Cramps: The symptoms are cramps in large muscles, usually following prolonged activity. They are relieved by rest and stretching.

Heat Exhaustion: This entity is more closely related to dehydration and has symptoms of dizziness or fainting, particularly when arising from a sitting or lying position. It may be accompanied by headache, nausea, vomiting, or generalized weakness. It also is treated by resting, avoiding further sun exposure, drinking plenty of fluids, and doing whatever necessary to cool down.

Heat Stroke: Heat stroke is the most serious of the heat-related illnesses. It can lead to death if not recognized and treated quickly. It is a condition during which the body loses its ability to control temperature, and the traveler's fever rises rapidly, often to levels of 105 degrees or higher. Symptoms, such as disorientation, confusion, and clumsiness, may appear without warning. Often the patient is unaware, but bystanders can detect that something is wrong. The temperature rises, and often the body loses its ability to sweat. Skin may appear flushed or reddened. Dehydration may also be present, though the major problem is the core temperature itself. As the condition progresses, seizures or coma may result.

The person must be taken to a cool environment away from the direct sun, and the body temperature must be lowered. Cold cloths, ice applied to the skin, fans, immersion in cold water, or any other method of lowering the body temperature must be used. Usually intravenous fluids are needed, but you should not wait for this treatment to begin lowering the temperature. Oral fluids should be started immediately. If the body temperature cannot be lowered quickly, brain, kidney, heart damage, and even death may occur.

This situation is one where the buddy system is useful. All mission team members should be paired with a buddy. Buddies monitor each other and watch each other for the symptoms of heat stroke. If your buddy suspects that you are becoming dehydrated or developing heat stroke, he should have the authority to command you to stop and rest.

Sunburn: Sunburn is as common as traveler's diarrhea in countries near the equator. Exposure may not become apparent until too late, so the traveler should always try to avoid direct sunlight when possible. Not only can exposure cause the immediate conditions of heat exhaustion and heat stroke (see above), but acute sunburn can ultimately lead to skin cancer years later (either less serious basal cell cancer or the more serious melanoma). Sunburn is caused by the ultraviolet light waves. Two types of ultraviolet light are UVA and UVB. UVA is the lesser culprit in sunburn. UVB causes the most damage to the skin. It is most dangerous during midday, near the equator, and at high altitudes. UVB is reflected, and water, snow, light-colored buildings, sand, or concrete surfaces may magnify its effect.

Your first defense against sunburn should be to avoid intense sunlight. Stay inside or under cover during peak sun intensity, and cover your skin with clothing, umbrellas, hats, and sunscreen (use SPF 15–40).

After you have experienced sunburn, aspirin or another non-steroidal anti-inflammatory agent, such as ibuprofen, may be useful. Cool showers may feel good. Severe cases may require an oral steroid, such as prednisone.

Sun-Induced Drug Reactions: Some medications sensitize the skin to sunlight, and exposure to sunlight may cause nasty reactions. Sun-induced drug reactions are particularly relevant to short-term mission trips because they often occur in tropical environments. Medications can cause one of two types of reactions— phototoxic and photoallergic. Phototoxic reactions are more common and resemble a sunburn in the timing of the symptoms and in the distribution of the reactions. The phototoxic reaction appears about thirty minutes after exposure and is identified by redness, swelling, and pain.

A photoallergic reaction is more of a true allergy in that it involves an immunologic mechanism; it requires previous exposure to the drug. A photoallergic reaction may not appear for up to two weeks, and it may appear initially as blisters without the redness that accompanies an ordinary sunburn. It may itch at first and may be confused with an eczema-type eruption. Treatment of both types of reactions is to minimize any further sun exposure and to stop taking the drug (if possible). To treat the affected skin, keep the area clean. Algesics and, in some circumstances, antihistamines or steroids may be needed. Persons taking offending medications should be aware of the problem and be more careful to avoid sun exposure.

Some Drugs and Chemicals Reported to Cause Photosensitivity:[20][21]
* particularly common or serious

ANTICANCER DRUGS
Actinomycin D
Dacarbazine
Doxorubicin
  hydrochloride
Fluorocytosin
Fluorouracil
Hydroxyurea
Methotrexate
Procarbazine
Vinblastine

ANTIDEPRESSANTS
Amitriptyline (Elavil)
Amoxapine
Chlorpromazine
  (Thorazine)
Desipramine
Doxepin (Sinequan)
Imipramine (Tofranil)
Isocarboxazid
Maprotiline
Nortriptyline
Protriptyline
Trimipramine

ANTIHISTAMINES
Carbinoxamine
Cyproheptadine
Diphenhydramine
  (Benadryl)

ANTIMICROBIALS
Chlortetracycline
Ciprofloxacin (Cipro)*
Declomycin*
Demeclocycline*
Doxycycline
Enoxacin*
Fansidar
Fleroxacin*
Griseofulvin
Lomefloxacin*
Methacycline
Minocycline (Minocin)
Nalidixic acid*
Norfloxacin (Norflox)*
Ofloxacin*
Oxytetracycline
Pefloxacin*
Sulfadoxine-
  pyrimethamine
Sulfamethizole
Sulfamethoxazole-
  trimethoprim (TMP-
  SMX, Septra,
  Bactrim)
Sulfasalazine
Sulfasoxazole
Tetracycline

ANTIPARASITIC DRUGS
Bithionol
Chloroquine
Pyrvinium pamoate
Quinine

ANTIPSYCHOTIC DRUGS
Chlordiazepoxide
  (Librium)*
Chlorpromazine*
Chlorprothixene
Fluphenazine
Haloperidol
Perphenazine
Piperacetazine
Prochlorperazine
Thioridazine (Mellaril)
Thiothixene
Tricyclic antidepressants
Trifluoperazine

DIURETICS
Acetazolamide (Diamox)
Amiloride
Bendroflumethiazide
Cyclothiazide
Chlorothiazide (Diuril)
Furosemide (Lasix)
Hydrochlorothiazide
  (Hydrodiuril)
Hydroflumethiazide
Methyclothiazide
Metolazone

Polythiazide
Quinethazone
Trichlormethiazide

HYPOGLYCEMICS
Acetohexamide
Chlorpropamide
Gilpizide
Glyburide
Tolazamide
Tolbumatide

*NONSTEROIDAL
ANTI-
INFLAMMATORY
DRUGS*
Ibuprofen
Ketoprofen
Carprofen
Naproxen
Phenylbutazone
Piroxicam
Sulindac

OTHER
Amiodarone
   (Cordarone,
   Pacerone)*
Barbiturates
Captopril (Capoten)
Carbamazepine
Clofazimine
Clofibrate
Coal tars
   (Tegrin, Denorex)

Cyclamates
Disopyramide
Estrogens
Etretinate
Gold salts
Fenofibrate
Hematoporphyrin
Hydralazine
Isoniazid
Isotretinoin
Oral contraceptives
Phenytoin
Progestins
Promethazine
Psoralen derivatives
Quinidine sulfate and
   gluconate (Quinidex,
   Quinaglute)
Trimeprazine
Triacetyldiphenolisatin

TOPICAL AGENTS
Para-aminobenzoic acid
   (PABA)
Benzocaine
Beta-carotene
Chlorhexidine
Coal tars
   (Tegrin, Denorex)
Dibucaine
Diphenhydramine
   (Benadryl)

Oils (bergamot, cedar,
  citron, lavender, lime,
  neroli, petitgrain,
  sandalwood)
Hexachlorophene
Hydrocortisone
Sulfanilamide

TETANUS

Tetanus is rare in most developed countries but may be seen in developing nations. Tetanus immunization boosters are recommended if you have not had one in the past ten years, but a booster is also recommended for any seriously dirty wound. Because no one can predict the type of wound that might be encountered on a trip, I recommend a booster if you have not had one for five years.

TRAVELER'S DIARRHEA

This ailment can afflict as many of one-half of all travelers.[22] About 20 percent of all mission team members will become bedridden from traveler's diarrhea, and 40 percent will need to change part of their trip because of the illness.[23] It has many causes, some bacterial, some viral, and some other causes. It is almost always transmitted by impure food or water. The organisms responsible for disease are usually transmitted by the oral-fecal route, often because a food handler does not wash his hands.

Prevention: Foods that are handled directly and then not fully cooked are particularly dangerous. Street vendors should always be avoided. Foods that grow in contact with the ground are also dangerous, and almost any vegetable can be contaminated. They should be washed and thoroughly disinfected (usually by soaking in chlorine water).

The best way to avoid traveler's diarrhea is to refuse to consume any questionable food or drink. The best guide for food consumption is "Peel it, boil it, cook it, or forget it!" That is, avoid all raw foods unless you peel it *yourself*. Don't eat salads, fresh vegetables, fresh fruits, or raw seafood. In fact, all seafood and shellfish are difficult to preserve without spoiling, so avoiding all seafood might be wise. It is also wise to avoid milk, ice cream, yogurt, or other dairy products (however, if they come in sealed, commercial containers and have been pasteurized, they are probably safe). The further you travel from large cities, the more cautious you should be. Usually the local missionary can help you steer clear of places where the food and water are bad.

A simple epidemiological principle is to limit the *sources* of your food and water. Water is always a potential source of danger. It may contain bacteria, viruses, and/or parasites. Obtain your water from a single source. Suppose you have the option of drinking water from four wells, and one of them is contaminated. If you drink water from only one well, you have at least a three-in-four chance that you will *not* be drinking bad water. If, on the other hand, you drink from all wells, you are certain to become ill. So you must limit the sources of what you consume. (On the other hand, don't allow yourself to become dehydrated. And remember that caffeine-containing beverages can act as diuretics, causing you to need even more fluids.)

Preventing traveler's diarrhea can be aided by medications. Pepto-Bismol is often recommended (the liquid form is more difficult to transport). Pepto-Bismol can cause some degree of constipation, it can turn stools black, it can cause a black tongue, and it may cause ringing in the ears. It contains salicylates, so a person allergic to aspirin or taking medications that interact with aspirin, such as warfarin (Coumadin), should not take Pepto-Bismol. Furthermore, Pepto-Bismol should not be taken for more than three weeks. Antibiotics, such as doxycycline (100 mg once daily), ciprofloxacin (500 mg once daily), norfloxacin (400 mg once daily), and trimethoprim-sulfa (one DS tablet daily) have all been studied. They are not recommended for routine prophylaxis because they may cause certain types of bowel infections. Furthermore, taking antibiotics can allow the overgrowth of vaginal yeasts, causing vaginal infections in females. Remember that all medications have side effects, some potentially serious. Most travel experts do not recommend routine antibiotics for travelers.

Symptoms: The symptoms of traveler's diarrhea are malaise, fever, abdominal cramps, and watery diarrhea (usually more than four or five loose, watery stools per day). Nausea and vomiting may also occur. Traveler's diarrhea most commonly occurs during the first week of travel but can appear at any time, even days after return to the United States. Traveler's diarrhea can leave a person feeling very fatigued and dizzy, and it may cause fainting if dehydration develops. Traveler's diarrhea usually lasts only two to four days, and it is *not* accompanied by a high fever, bloody diarrhea, or mucous in the stools. Any of these latter symptoms should prompt the traveler to seek immediate medical attention. Chronic diarrhea after return from a mission trip (often accompanied by bloating, nondescript abdominal pain, and weight loss) usually means that the traveler has contracted another kind of illness and should seek a medical evaluation. Again many physicians are not familiar with exotic infectious diseases, and it may be necessary to see an infectious disease specialist or to be evaluated at a travel and tropical medicine clinic.

Treatment: Treatment for traveler's diarrhea is easier to describe than to accomplish. Since most cases last only a few days, the simplest and safest treatment is simply to not travel while feeling ill, to lie down and rest, to drink plenty of fluids, to take aspirin or acetaminophen for fever, and to wait for the illness to pass. Avoid acidic fluids (citrus drinks, for example) and milk. Try to rest. Most short-term mission trips are characterized by a need to be at certain places at specific times, to accomplish a task. It may be impossible to rest if the day's schedule calls for the entire group to board a train and travel far into the innards of sub-Saharan Africa or to catch a flight to Siberia that goes only once each week. All teams should carry an anti-motility agent and an antibiotic. In such circumstances, an antidiarrheal, (such as loperamide (Imodium) or diphenoxylate (Lomotil)—4 mg followed by 2 mg after each loose stool up to 16 mg daily) is in order, even though it is not routinely recommended. Other useful medicines are the opiates (paregoric, codeine). These medications should not be used if you have high fever or bloody stools; these symptoms mean that you should consult with a physician immediately.

Antibiotics are sometimes used to treat *established* traveler's diarrhea in addition to being used for prevention. The drugs mentioned above are all useful for mild to moderate symptoms: ciprofloxacin (a single dose of 750 mg), trimethoprim-sulfa (one double-strength tablet daily), doxycycline (100 mg daily), norfloxacin, levofloxacin (a single dose of 500 mg), ofloxacin (a single dose of 400 mg), and azithromycin (one 500 mg. tablet daily). Severe symptoms can be treated with ciprofloxacin (500 mg. twice daily for three days), levofloxacin (500 mg daily for three days), norfloxacin (400 mg twice daily for three days), ofloxacin (300 mg twice daily for three days), or azithromycin (1000 mg once; or 500 mg on day one then 250 mg daily for four days). These medications should not be used for illnesses characterized only by nausea and vomiting without diarrhea.

Be careful to avoid dehydration. Use oral rehydration solutions if necessary. Such solutions may be unpleasant tasting and adding small amounts of Jell-O or Kool-Aid powder may make them more palatable, especially for children. Small amounts frequently taken are sufficient, though it is almost impossible to give too much fluids. Another method of rehydration involves drinking two types of liquids: one contains eight ounces of fruit juice, 1/2 teaspoon of honey or corn syrup, and a pinch of salt; the second is eight ounces of purified or carbonated water and 1/2 teaspoon of baking soda. The patient should sip alternately from each solution until no longer thirsty.[24]

Foods that aid in slowing diarrhea are rice, wheat products, potatoes, toast, bananas, corn, and chicken. Though foods containing acidophilus or lactobacillus cultures may be useful after return home (foods such as milk, yogurt, or powders containing these cultures), these foods are often contaminated in foreign countries.

TUBERCULOSIS

Tuberculosis is a bacterial disease spread by droplet contamination (a cough or sneeze) from an infected person. It may be much more common in the area where you are going than in the United States. It takes a long time (weeks or months) to incubate, so symptoms will appear only after you have returned from the foreign land. Tuberculin skin testing is advisable as a screening technique prior to the trip.

TYPHOID FEVER

Typhoid affects approximately three to thirty persons per 100,000 travelers per month to developing countries.[25] The symptoms include fevers that progressively worsen from day to day, headache, fatigue, and flu-like symptoms. The fevers may reach 103 to 104 degrees F and remain elevated. As the illness progresses, either diarrhea or constipation may develop. Serious complications include intestinal perforation with severe abdominal pain, distention, and low blood pressure. Death may result in untreated cases. A person can carry the disease though not have any symptoms; thus, it can be passed to others unknowingly. Typhoid vaccine can be given either orally or intramuscularly. The oral form requires four doses given every other day, and it lasts five years. There are two forms given by injection. One is given in two doses four weeks apart, lasting three years, and the other given as a single dose lasting two years.

VENOUS THROMBOSIS

Prolonged inactivity can lead to blood clots in the lower extremities. These clots may cause no symptoms, though they can produce calf or leg pain and swelling of the ankles or calves. To prevent these clots, you should walk around as frequently as possible and avoid dehydration, which means avoiding caffeine and alcohol, which you should avoid anyway.

YELLOW FEVER

Yellow fever is also transmitted by a mosquito bite. It is endemic to Central Africa and Central and South America in regions near the equator. It usually begins three to six days after the bite, and the symptoms are fever, malaise, lower back pain, nausea, and vomiting. A rash may appear, and more severe cases result in jaundice—the reason it is called yellow fever. Serious cases can cause seizures, confusion, and coma. There is no specific treatment for yellow fever, though a vaccination is available. Anyone traveling to an endemic area should take the immunization, which requires a booster every ten years.

Sample List of Medical Exposures

Because many illnesses may not manifest themselves until team members have returned to the United States, it may be useful for team members to have a list of potential exposures with them so that they can give the list to a doctor. This is an example of a list I made to give to the team that recently worked with me in Honduras.

Summary of Medical Exposures
Balfate, Honduras
July 2000

Teams serving Hospital Loma de Luz in Balfate, Colon, Honduras, have been exposed to many illnesses, some of which are uncommon in the United States. Upon return to the States, the team members and their physicians should be aware of these exposures in case of illness upon return home. Below are summaries of some illnesses of the region:

Malaria

Malaria is present in the Balfate region, though not prevalent. Two presumptive cases were seen in the Loma de Luz Clinic in Hondurans during the team's tenure here. Not all team members were taking prophylactic chloroquin.

Symptoms: otherwise unexplained fever, generalized body aches (especially muscle aches and bone pain), headache

Incubation period: usually one to three weeks, but it can be up to one year

Dengue

More dengue than malaria has been seen in the Balfate area. Three of the four adult missionaries here have had dengue in the last year. Dengue is transmitted by the bite of a mosquito.

Symptoms: fever, severe eye pain, headache, severe bone and muscle pain.

Incubation period: two to seven days

Leishmaniasis

Cutaneous leishmaniasis is also endemic to the region. The north shore has predominantly cutaneous leishmaniasis, though muco-cutaneous and visceral forms are also seen further inland. One case was seen in the clinic during the team's stay. It is transmitted by bites of the sandfly, and virtually all team members experienced such bites.

Symptoms: papules that itch and then later develop ulcers

Incubation period: up to eight weeks

Intestinal parasites

Nearly 100 percent of the permanent residents of the Balfate area have infestation with roundworms as well as other intestinal parasites. The team's diet and water supply were relatively well controlled, and we do not expect them to develop such infestation. Prophylactic treatment with mebendazole or albendazole after returning home is probably not necessary.

Symptoms: vague abdominal complaints, abdominal pain, passing a worm, cough, fever

Incubation period: weeks to months, in some cases up to one year

Amebiasis

Amebiasis has been a real problem in this region, especially for the North American missionaries. Water for the team was always commercially purified and extra chlorine was always added. Nevertheless, amebiasis is a distinct possibility after residence here for even a few days.

Symptoms: abdominal pain, diarrhea, even fever with more severe cases

Incubation period: usually two to six weeks

Viral URI's

The most common illness seen in the clinic was the viral URI syndrome. It seems to be a particularly stubborn variety, with persistent cough and sore throat, sometimes lasting weeks.

Symptoms: sore throat, fever, cough

Incubation period: three to seven days

Tick bites

Ticks are abundant here, and many team members experienced more than one bite. In contrast to tick bites in the U.S., there have been no diseases identified locally that are carried by Honduran ticks. Lyme disease has not been recognized in the Balfate region, and the rickettsial diseases (e.g. Rocky Mountain spotted fever) have not been seen. The bites elicit an intense allergic response often leaving an itchy lesion that may persist for months.

Symptoms: tick discovered on the skin, itchy lesion

Incubation period: symptoms appear as soon as the bite occurs.

Leptospirosis

Leptospirosis is also present here, and the most of the team went swimming in both the ocean and in a fresh water stream.

Symptoms: fever, chills, headache, nausea, vomiting, myalgias

Incubation period: two to twenty-six days

Typhoid fever

One case of presumed typhoid fever was seen in the region during the team's stay.

Symptoms: fever, headache, abdominal pain and tenderness, skin rash

Incubation period: eight to fourteen days

Cholera

Isolated cases of cholera have recently been reported in both Honduras and Guatemala, but there have been none in the local region.

Symptoms: abdominal cramps, nausea, vomiting, profuse diarrhea

Incubation period: one to several days

Skin diseases

Many contact allergens are part of the environment on the north shore of Honduras. Most have not been identified. Many of the team members developed skin rashes, usually on the exposed regions of the skin. Some persons developed lower extremity edema, unusual ecchymosis, and one had frank cellulitis. The exact cause was never identified.

Symptoms: itchy rash

Incubation period: one or two days

This list is not intended to be inclusive but simply to summarize the prevalent illnesses in Honduras to which the team might have been exposed.

Leon Greene, M.D.

Appendix F

IMMUNIZATIONS

It is crucial to maintain a complete immunization schedule (measles, mumps rubella, polio, pertussis, diphtheria, tetanus, hepatitis A, hepatitis B, influenza, varicella, and Haemophilus type b) and to obtain immunizations for diseases endemic to the area *before* you travel on your mission assignment. It's too late to decide that you need an immunization after you've landed in the Congo, where obtaining the correct shot may be costly, impossible, or even dangerous (if injections are not performed with clean, sterile equipment). There is no substitute for individual consultation with your personal physician or a physician well versed in travel medicine. This appendix[26] is merely a summary of immunizations You should *visit your physician at least 6 months prior to the mission trip* to allow time for appropriate immunizations.

Recommendations for immunizations are frequently changed, and the best source for up-to-date schedules can be found at www.cdc.gov/travel. You should first go to this web site to learn about the diseases to which you might be exposed during your trip.

Certain conditions require additional precautions and immunizations. Patients at higher risk for disease are people with the following conditions:

- Pregnancy
- Diabetes
- Chronic heart conditions
- Chronic lung conditions
- Chronic liver disease (including alcoholism)
- Chronic kidney disease
- Immunodeficiency, including HIV infection
- Cancer
- People who have had their spleen removed, been treated with immunosuppressive drugs or steroids, and have experienced large doses of radiation exposure are also at a higher risk.

Depending upon the expected exposure, recommendations for travel immunization will differ. The missionary on the streets of Paris will have better access to medical care than the missionary to Rwanda. The following Tables outline both general and routine missionary service immunizations for reference:

Immunizations Recommended for General Missionary Travel *

	Schedule	Duration of effect	Booster before travel
Cholera	1-3 doses over 2-4 weeks	6 months-2 years	If more than 6 months since last dose
Cholera immunization is quite ineffective and generally not recommended. Schedule is dependent on the type of immunization administered. Very few countries still require documentation of immunization for entry.			
Meningitis	1 dose	3-5 years	If more than 3 years since last dose
For travelers to endemic/epidemic areas only.			
Typhoid fever	Oral 1 capsule every other day for 4 doses, or IM 1-2 doses 4 weeks apart	5 years oral, 2-3 years IM	If more than 5 years since last oral dose, or 2 years since last IM dose
This immunization is recommended if your travel takes you to remote areas with poor sanitation. Immunization can be IM or oral.			
Yellow fever	1 dose	10 years	If more than 10 since last dose
Only as required in endemic areas.			
Malaria	Not applicable	Not applicable	Not applicable
See Appendix E. No immunization exists against malaria. Prophylaxis depends on taking oral medication before, during, and after the trip.			
Rabies	3 doses over 3 weeks	6-36 months	If more than 6-36 months since last dose, depending on risk
Rabies immunization is recommended for persons traveling to endemic areas for more than 6 months, those exposed to animals for over 1 month, or those in high-risk areas for over 1 month.			
Japanese Encephalitis	3 doses over 1 month	3 years	If more than 3 years since last dose
For travel to endemic areas only.			
Lyme disease	3 doses over 1 year	Unknown, perhaps 1 year	
Not routinely administered.			
Plague	3 doses over 6 months	1-2 years	If more than 1 year since last dose
For selected regions only.			
Smallpox	1 dose	? lifetime	
Smallpox vaccinations were discontinued in the 1970s, but recent terrorist threats have raised the concern over this disease. At the time of the printing of this book, smallpox vaccinations were still not being offered to the general public.			

*None of these immunizations are routine in the United States

IM = intramuscular

Routine Immunizations
(Everyone should have already received these.)

	Birth-2 weeks	2 mos	4 mos	6 mos	12-15 mos	15-18 mos	4-6 yrs	10-12 yrs	14-16 yrs	Routine Schedule	Duration of Effect	Booster Before Travel
Diptheria, Pertussis (Whooping Cough), Tetanus		X	X	X		X	X			TD every 10 years	T is 5-10 years	T or TD
General recommendations include giving a booster shot for a dirty or complicated ("tetanus-prone") wound. I usually recommend a tetanus booster before missionary travel as a precaution, especially if you have not had one in the last 5 years. If you need one on a trip, it could be difficult to obtain in a foreign country.												
Poliomyelitis		X	X	X			X			1 booster as adult		
Inactivated, injected polio vaccine is the current recommendation (as opposed to oral live polio vaccine).												
Measles, Mumps, Rubella					X		X			2 in lifetime	Lifetime	
No adult booster required.												
Haemophilus influenza type b		X	X	X	X					4 in lifetime	Lifetime	
No adult booster required.												

Hepatitis B	X	X	X			3 over 6 months	Not known, possibly lifetime

Many adults have not had this immunization, and it is recommended.

Hepatitis A				X		2 over 6 months	Not known / If more than 10 years

Many adults have not had this immunization, and it is recommended, especially for missionary travel. Full protection is present 14 days after last injection. A booster might be needed after 10 years.

Varicella			X				

Recommended for persons without well-documented history of varicella (chicken pox). If under 13 years of age, 1 dose is recommended; if over 13 years, 2 doses separated by 4-8 weeks is recommended.

Pneumococcal conjugate	X	X	X			1 dose PPV	PPV if more than 5 years

Pneumococcal conjugate vaccine is given to children. Pneumococcal polysaccharide vaccine is recommended for adults.

Influenza						Yearly	Yearly

Strain of predominant virus changes frequently. Yearly dose recommended.

T = tetanus

PPV = pneumococcal polysaccharide vaccine

235

Many diseases have no effective immunization, for example, malaria. Prevention is dependent upon taking an oral medication before, during, and after the trip. Other diseases (like dengue) have no preventive medication or immunization and avoiding them depends upon minimizing the exposure to the vector of transmission (the mosquito). You should try to minimize your exposure to such insects to the extent reasonably possible (see Appendix E, "How to Stay Healthy"). Similar illnesses carried by known vectors are African sleeping sickness (transmitted by the tsetse fly), Chagas' disease (transmitted by the reduvid bug), many kinds of encephalitis (transmitted by mosquitoes), leishmaniasis (transmitted by sand flies), plague (transmitted by fleas, though a vaccine is available against this disease), and schistosomiasis (carried in impure water).

Appendix G

EMERGENCY PLANS AND DISASTER RELIEF

Disasters may strike anywhere, and a missionary may be thrust into a disaster situation only to find himself in charge. The areas where missionaries work are needy by definition—often both spiritually and physically. Practical demonstrations of the love of Christ may include assisting someone in the face of a disaster. The missionary may be the best-educated person in the region and may also have the most contacts and resources to deal with a calamity. The same is true of short-term missionaries.

For the most part, the types of disasters to which we might be exposed on the mission field can be predicted. Common sense tells us that if we live near a volcano, a volcanic eruption would be one type of expected danger. Certain political climates could predict the possibility of a war or a refugee situation. Studying the history of the region might tell us what disasters we could encounter and what types of injuries and needs we should expect.

Many accidents or illnesses you may encounter are commonplace and can be avoided with a little caution and preparation. When asked what is the most common cause of death among short-term missionaries, most people respond with exotic diseases. "Ebola virus!" "Tsutsugamushi!" But the answer is rather mundane: automobile accidents. For some reason, Westerners throw caution to the wind when visiting a foreign culture. Seat belts go unused. Youth ride in the back of an open pickup truck, which, of course, has poor brakes, no shocks, and is driven too fast on roads that resemble the Oregon Trail. What is the most common preventable infectious disease? Malaria. We forget to take our weekly malaria pills. The most common medical illness is hepatitis, which could be prevented by immunization. The most common cause of preventable disability is traveler's diarrhea. We forget and drink the local water, which may have come from the local river. These items, and others, are covered in Appendix E on staying healthy.

Often short-term medical and relief missions are actually targeted toward disaster sites. Members of a short-term mission (as well as the full-time missionaries) should have well-defined plans for medical and other types of emergencies. The local hospital or emergency room may be substandard, out of commission, or non-existent, so team members must know what to do in the event of a serious medical illness or injury. Is it adequate to use the local facilities, or is evacuation necessary? In this appendix you will find an outline of some of the principles you should consider when planning for your emergency plans and disaster relief.

Preparation for a disaster can take two forms: (1) preparation for your mission team and (2) preparation for assisting the entire community as a disaster relief agent. Preparation is especially important for those short-term mission teams going to an area where a disaster has already occurred. Certainly, you should prepare for your own team, but as an agent of God, you should also plan carefully how you are going to assist the community.

While we cannot stockpile enough food and water for the entire community, perhaps not even for our own team or immediate neighbors, we can be prepared by assessing the potential sources of supplies in our region, as well as the nearby areas.

Though we are not to be consumed with worries about the future, we can be prepared for adverse events in our lives and in the lives of others. By so doing, we can also be helpful and minister to our neighbors.

What types of emergencies might we expect? A simple assessment of our destination, its climate, and the political and environmental exposure can provide a hint of possible future calamities.

1. Types of emergencies and accidents
   a. Automobile accidents or other trauma
   b. Heat-related illnesses
   c. Infectious diseases (food-borne, waterborne, and insect-borne)
   d. Altitude-related illnesses
   e. Skin diseases
   f. Travel-related illnesses (motion sickness, jet lag)
   g. Other (bites, envenomations)

2. Natural disasters
   a. Earthquake
   b. Flood
   c. Volcano
   d. Tornado
   e. Hurricane, monsoon, cyclone
   f. Tidal wave, tsunami
   g. Etc.

3. Man made disasters
   a. Political, governmental coup
   b. War

c. Terrorism (bombs, explosions, chemical or biological agents)
d. Riots
e. Nuclear accident
f. Chemical spill
g. Industrial explosion

Responding to an Emergency or Disaster

Preparation for disasters entails the same type of planning for most all events listed above. You should, of course, cover all your activities with prayer, both before and after the event. The basic disaster planning principles include education, prevention, mitigation, and general preparation. After a disaster occurs, the principles include search and rescue, rehabilitation, reconstruction, and mitigation against future events.

The response after any disaster includes setting priorities for action: (1) family and mission community, (2) immediate neighborhood, and (3) the larger population. You should plan a rapid assessment of needs by visual inspection, talking with community sources and relief personnel, and keeping abreast of press reports or local news. Reports to authorities should include the geographical area affected, the population, access, transportation, communication, and needs (estimates of food needs and available supplies, water needs, healthcare, clothing, shelter, sanitation, transportation, and fuel or power). The scope of damage should include the number dead, number injured, number missing, number displaced and location, urgent needs and materials, and resources available in the area. Relief workers need to monitor potential illnesses: diarrheal diseases, malaria, measles, tuberculosis, scabies, respiratory diseases, meningitis, parasitic diseases, anemia, tetanus, and longer-term problems such as vitamin deficiencies and the need for immunizations.

The team leaders should know evacuation procedures and routes, and emergency supplies should be readily available (fire extinguishers, flashlights, battery-powered radios, first aid kits, food and water, medications, fuel, etc.). The leaders or local missionaries should already have identified local disaster relief officials and local sources of medical care and communicated with them. Local cell phone networks and/or shortwave radio networks are invaluable but difficult to access after the disaster has begun. All of this integration with local officials should be done before calamity strikes.

Food and water supplies should be a first priority. Of course, it is impossible to supply entire communities or towns with food and water at the time of a disaster, but the mission team leader should know sources for both the missionaries and the short-term team. Water is the primary consideration (we can live longer without food than without water). Water purification is discussed in Appendix E. In general, the average adult in the tropics requires six liters per day (less in cooler climates). Food needs likewise depend on the climate and your activity, but the following table[27] summarizes average needs:

Age Group (years)	Height (cm.)	Emergency subsistence (for a few weeks): kcal / day	Temporary subsistence (for many months): kcal / day
0-1	Under 75	800	800
1-3	75-96	1100	1300
4-6	96-117	1300	1600
7-9	117-136	1500	1800
10 and over Male Female		1700 1500	2000 1800
Pregnant or lactating woman		1900	2200

The average adult needs an average of 1700 kcal per day to avoid starvation (preferably 3000 kcal for males and 2200 kcal for females). This requires 3–4 kg per week per person (basic rice, corn, wheat flour, or beans). For example, a daily ration might be rice (400 grams), fat (15 grams), and protein-rich food (45 grams). One cup of dry rice cooks to about 670 kilocalories; one cup of dry beans cooks to about 240 kilocalories.

Immunizations should have been obtained prior to your trip. In general and contrary to popular belief, immunizations for both the visiting team and the local population *after the disaster* are a relatively low priority.

The disaster may foster gastrointestinal diseases characterized by diarrhea and dehydration, particularly in infants and children. Treatment consists primarily of oral rehydration solutions (intravenous solutions are rarely necessary). These can be obtained from the World Health Organization or from commercial manufacturers (such as Pedialyte™). The solution can be homemade from the following ingredients:

- 1 liter of pure water
- 2 tablespoons of sugar
- 1/4 teaspoon of salt
- 1/4 teaspoon of bicarbonate of soda

or, more simply,

- one glass of pure water
- a pinch of salt
- a teaspoon of sugar

(Note: These formulas do not contain potassium, which is necessary and included in the pre-packaged solutions.)

Shelter often must include mass housing for local residents, and many times it is temporarily provided by schools, churches, and other large facilities. Temporary facilities may also include tents or tarps. Clothing and blankets must come from local sources, at least for the first few days. Sanitation often must be primitive latrines. Transportation and fuel must also originate locally.

Relief work involves identifying special populations who at particular risk from the disaster, such as children, elderly, physically or mentally challenged persons, and people who are chronically ill or malnourished.

Preparation for Specific Disasters

Specific preparations for natural disasters are dependent on the expected event.

Earthquake: Earthquake preparation includes securing shelves, heavy objects, furniture, and appliances to the walls. These procedures are familiar to most schoolchildren in the United States: if indoors, take cover under sturdy furniture and stay inside; if outside, move into the open; and if in a vehicle, move away from buildings, trees, overpasses, or utility lines, and stop the vehicle and stay inside. After the earthquake, be prepared for aftershocks, stay out of damaged buildings, and don't return home until authorities have declared it to be safe. Avoid dangling power lines and report them to the authorities. Clean up flammable liquids immediately. Open all doors and closets carefully, and check structure for damage.

Flood: For floods, identify sources of, or stockpile, sandbags, shovels, sand, plywood, plastic sheeting, nails, and hammers. Locate turn-off valves for water, sewage, electricity, and gas. Identify evacuation routes. Fill large containers (sinks, bathtubs, etc.) with clean water. Move possessions to high ground, as appropriate. Turn off electricity and gas. Evacuate, but never drive a car through floodwaters—this is the most common cause of fatalities during a flood. After the flood, examine structures for damage and avoid areas exposing you to the danger of electric shock or a gas explosion. Be cautious about poisonous animals that may have been displaced by the flood. Discard any food that was damaged by floodwaters.

Volcano: In the case of a volcano, identify warning signs and signals of impending eruption. Be aware that volcanoes can cause floods, mudslides, landslides, tsunamis, and can be associated with earthquakes. Obtain breathing masks and goggles. Identify evacuation routes. Acutely move out of the downwind region of the eruption, if possible. Seek high ground. Close windows, doors, and dampers. Seek shelter indoors. Wear goggles and masks. After the eruption, avoid ash fall and maintain goggles and masks until air is clear.

Tornado: During a tornado, go to a basement, cellar, storm shelter, or the lowest level of the building. If you don't have access to any of these options, go to an inner hallway. Stay away from windows and outside walls, and get under a sturdy piece of furniture. After the tornado, inspect for electrical and gas problems and for sewer and water line damage

Hurricane: In the event of a hurricane, monsoon, or cyclone, install shutters or board windows, and trim trees that could fall on your home. Fill large containers (sinks, bathtubs, etc.) with water. Bring outdoor items that aren't secure into a house or garage. Turn the refrigerator to the coldest setting, and open only when necessary. Stay away from windows, skylights, and glass doors. Evacuate, if instructed to do so. After the hurricane, return home only after authorities have declared it to be safe. Avoid dangling power lines and report them to the authorities. Be cautious about poisonous animals that may have been displaced by the hurricane. Discard any food that was damaged by water.

Landslide, mudflow, or avalanche: After a landslide, mudflow, or avalanche, plant ground cover on sloping land and build retaining walls. Learn to recognize the warning signs of an impending landslide (doors or windows suddenly begin to jam or stick; new cracks in walls, plaster, tile, brick, or foundations; cracks begin to enlarge; underground pipes or utilities break; ground at the base of a slope is bulging; new water springs develop; there is movement of retaining walls, fences, poles, trees, rumbling sounds). If indoors, stay inside and take cover under sturdy furniture. If outdoors, escape the path of the landslide or mudflow and get to high ground. Seek shelter from rocks and debris. After the landslide or mudflow, avoid the slide area and be alert for floods. Check for damaged utility lines, power cables, etc. Check structural integrity of the building

Man-made disasters: Man-made disasters have achieved a new significance since September 11, 2001. We have become more aware of the risk of chemical, biological, and nuclear terrorism. Other sources of calamity include political coups, insurrections, riots, wars, arsons, shootings, and industrial accidents or explosions. Guarding against terrorism has become a full-time job for many, though success in preventing these disasters is elusive. Terrorists seek both to inflict damage and to produce fear in the population. High visibility targets with a large opportunity for mass casualties are most vulnerable. The terrorists' willingness to sacrifice their own lives makes protection of sites very difficult. The major defense is to remain alert for suspicious activity and to avoid crowded locations. Our real responses to terrorists should be these:

Terrorists come to our country to kill and destroy. We should be willing to go to theirs to witness and heal.

Terrorists are willing to die for their religion. We should be willing to live for ours.

Summary[28]

Do
- Consult with disaster authorities
- Request cash if aid is needed. Most needed items can be purchased in nearby non-affected regions or countries
- Continue to help in all phases listed above
- Coordinate all agencies
- Consult authorities on needs for equipment, tents, food, vaccines, etc.

Don't
- Encourage donations of used clothing, food from afar, household medications or personal prescriptions, or blood products.
- Ask for field hospitals or medical teams (unless health authorities agree; if so, help from nearby countries is preferable).

"Whatever you do, the victims of a disaster are on their own for at least several hours after a sudden disaster. Victims are rescued by other victims, not by rescue teams. . . . They have to care for the initial search and rescue, the initial feeding of the affected populations as well as for providing initial information on damage and needs." —Phillipe Boulle, United Nations Disaster Response Organization [29]

"Time is the most valuable and limited resource disaster relief managers have in any major disaster. Every moment counts. Human suffering increases whenever relief work is needlessly delayed. The biggest waste of precious time we must invariably deal with in every disaster visible to the public is unsolicited, inappropriate and unneeded relief commodities. Educating the American public to channel their admirable humanitarian instincts into more productive routes remains one of our most serious challenges. Every level of American interest, including politicians, academicians, church groups and ethnic associations must practice sound judgment and discipline in their efforts to respond appropriately to needs of victims of disasters." —Andrew Natsios, U.S. Office of Foreign Disaster Assistance[30]

"The local population is in the best position to understand its own environment and culture and consequently it is able to provide not only a quicker but also a more adequate response to disasters.

"Preparedness experiences in small communities in Latin America and the Caribbean demonstrate that to be motivated to prepare for disasters, people must be convinced that reducing their vulnerability contributes to the overall development of the community, since disasters only worsen the day-to-day problems of poverty and underdevelopment. In small communities the lesson was learned that it is not possible to consider the link between disasters on the one hand and health on the other, without addressing comprehensive socioeconomic development as a whole."[31]

Appendix H

USEFUL WEB SITES

- World missions

    U.S. Center for World Missions—www.missionfrontiers.org—The premier organization for world evangelization. The U.S. site is www.uscwm.org.

- Short-term missions

    Medical Missions—www.medmissions.org—is a site maintained by a physician in Honduras. It lists many planned short-term outreaches, especially medically oriented ones in Latin America.

    Christian Medical and Dental Association—www.cmds.org—has two types of mission programs. One is for delivering medical care, Global Health Outreach/Medical Group Missions, and the other is for medical professionals who would like to teach medical topics, Commission On International Medical Education Affairs (COIMEA).

Interdenominational Foreign Missions Association of North America—www.ifmamissions.org—lists many foreign missions opportunities.

Operation Mobilization—www.om.org—provides links to short-term mission opportunities around the world.

Youth With A Mission—www.uofnkona.edu—provides a connection to one of the largest short-term missions groups. It is said to send over 100,000 persons per year on short-term missions.

Nazarenes—www.nazarene.org

Baptists—www.imb.org

Child Evangelism Fellowship—www.cefinc.org

Northwest Medical Teams—www.nwmti.org

General Information—www.shorttermmissions.com This site has many useful links to short-term organizations.

- Health-related information

    Centers for Disease Control—www.cdc.gov/travel. This site addresses what diseases are where and is very up to date. It should be your first place to check for questions about your country. It includes vaccination requirements, news of recent epidemics, and other useful travel information. www.cdc.gov/travel/destinat.htm has a map that you can click or lists areas of the world for you to click on a region or country.

World Health Organization—www.who.org (also www.who.int or www.who.ch)—lists diseases and recent outbreaks. It is more oriented to the medical professional.

Travel Health Information Service— www.travelhealth.com—has a great site with travel tips, medical information, and some great images.

Travel Health Online—www.tripprep.com/ index.html—displays each country and explains what diseases you might expect there and how to avoid the endemic diseases.

International Association for Medical Assistance to Travelers—www.cybermall.co.nz/NZ/ IAMAT—lists doctors, hospitals, and clinics in foreign lands.

International SOS Assistance— www.intsos.com—gives information on doctors and emergency care in foreign countries.

ProMED—www.fas.org/promed—lists disease outbreaks.

American Society of Tropical Medicine and Hygiene—www.astmh.org

International Society of Travel Medicine— www.istm.org

Travel Medicine—www.travmed.com

Health Canada Online—www.hc-sc.gc.ca

Canadian Society for International Health—www.csih.org

Wilderness Medical Society—www.wms.org

Medicine Planet—www.travelhealth.com

Immunization Action Coalition—www.immunize.org

Other immunization information—www.access1.net/via

International Association of Medical Assistance for Travelers—www.iamat.sentex.com

- Information about destination countries

    Central Intelligence Agency—www.odci.gov/cia/publications/pubs.html

    U.S. State Department—travel.state.gov. This government site lists countries and the dangers in each, as well as information on passports, tips for travelers by country, lists of doctors and hospitals in foreign countries, and travel warnings by country.

    Association for Safe International Road Travel—www.asirt.org—lists road travel conditions in over sixty countries.

- Disaster and emergency information

    American Red Cross—www.redcross.org/disaster/safety

    Pan American Health Organization—www.paho.org

    Federal Emergency Management Agency—www.fema.gov

    Disaster Relief—www.disasterrelief.org/EarthWatch

    Disaster News Network—www.disasternews.net/

    World Health Organization—www.who.int/eha/disasters

- Specific issues

    Water purification—www.rei.com. This site has reviews of water purification techniques, filters, etc.

    Travel Medicine, Inc.—www.travmed.com—sells medical supplies, repellents, water filters, etc.

- Passport information

    Department of State—travel.state.gov/passport_services.html—tells you how to obtain a passport. Visa.his.com tells you where to obtain one.

Appendix I

GOOD BOOKS ON MISSIONS

(Modified from a list compiled by Doug Nichols)[32]

   ☆   Very important
  ☆ ☆   A must
☆ ☆ ☆   Possibly one of the best

BIOGRAPHIES

A Chance to Die: The Life and Legacy of Amy Carmichael
By Elisabeth Elliot
Fleming H. Revell Company (1987), 382 pp.
☆ ☆ ☆

Adoniram Judson: America's First Foreign Missionary
By Faith Cox Bailey
Northfield Pub. (1999), 128 pp.
☆

Amy Carmichael: Let the Little Children Come
Lois Hoadley Dick
Moody Press (1984), 160 pp.
☆ ☆

Bruchko
By Bruce Olson
Creation House (1989), 208 pp.
☆ (Autobiography of Bruce Olson.)

Faithful Witness: The Life and Mission of William Carey
By Timothy George
Christian History Inst. (1998), 265 pp.
☆

Five Pioneer Missionaries
By John Thornbury, John D. Legg,
and R. Strang Miller
Banner of Truth (1991), 345 pp.
☆☆☆

From Jerusalem to Irian Jaya:
A Biographical History of Christian Missions
By Ruth Tucker
Zondervan (1983), 512 pp.
☆☆ (Biographies of ninety-nine key missionaries.)

Gladys Aylward: The Courageous English Missionary
By Catherine Swift
Bethany House (1989), 128 pp.
☆

Isobel Kuhn: Missionary to the Lisu in China
By Lois Hoadley Dick
Bethany House (1987), 157 pp.
☆

John G. Patton, Missionary to the New Hebrides (Vanuatu)
By John G. Patton
Banner of Truth (out of print), 524 pp.
☆☆

The Life and Diary of David Brainerd
By Philip E. Howard,
Jonathan Edwards, ed., and David Brainerd
Baker (1989), 385 pp.
☆☆

A Man in Christ: The Story of J. Hudson Taylor
By Roger Steer
Harold Shaw, 374 pp.
★★★ (One of the best biographies in print today!)

Mary Slessor: Heroine of the Calabar
By Basil Miller
Bethany House (1985), 139 pp.
★

No Sacrifice Too Great: The Story of C.T. Studd & Priscilla
By Eileen Vincent
WEC Publications, 253 pp.
★★ (Even with his faults, we can learn much from and praise God for C.T. Studd!)

Shadow of the Almighty: The Life & Testament of Jim Elliot
By Elisabeth Elliot
HarperSanFrancisco (reissue 1989), 256 pp.
★

Storming the Golden Kingdom:
Adoniram Judson, Apostle to Burma
By John Waters
InterVarsity Press (1989), 190 pp.
★★

William Carey: Pioneer Missionary to India
By Kellsye Finnie
Last published by OM Publishing (1987), 157 pp.
★★

William Carey
By Basil Miller
Bethany House (1985), 152 pp.
★★

GENERAL

A Biblical Theology of Missions
By George W. Peters
Moody Press (1972), 368 pp.
☆

Catch the Vision 2000
By Bill Stearns and Amy Stearns
Bethany House (1991), 206 pp.
☆

The Church Is Bigger Than You Think:
The Unfinished Work of World Evangelization
By Patrick Johnstone
Christian Focus (1998), 314 pp.
☆☆☆ (Excellent update on the task of the church.)

Communicating Cross-Culturally, Second Ed.:
An Introduction to Missionary Communication
By David J. Hesselgrave
Zondervan (1991), 672 pp.
☆

Crisis and Hope in Latin America: An Evangelical Perspective
By Emilio Antonio Núñez C.
Gabriel Resources (1996), 526 pp.
☆☆

Cross-Cultural Conflict:
Building Relationships for Effective Ministry
By Duane Elmer
InterVarsity Press (1994), 189 pp.
☆

Eternity in Their Hearts: Startling Evidence of Belief in the One True God in Hundreds of Cultures Throughout the World
By Don Richardson
Regal (1994), 223 pp.
☆

Go and Make Disciples! An Introduction to Christian Missions
By Roger S. Greenway
P&R Publishing (1990), 190 pp.
✫✫✫ (Excellent challenge.)

God's Call to Mission
By David Shenk
Herald Press (1994), 229 pp.
✫

Good News About Injustice:
A Witness of Courage in a Hurting World
By Gary Haugen
InterVarsity Press (1999), 201 pp.
✫ (Practical steps for dealing with injustice in the world.)

The Great Commission Lifestyle:
Conforming Your Life to Kingdom Priorities
By Robert Coleman
Fleming H Revell C. (1992), 126 pp.
✫

Honey, We're Going to Africa
By Harvey Thomas Hoekstra
Winepress (1995), 378 pp.
✫ (Out of print but available through William Carey Library.)

How to Be a World-Class Christian:
You Can Be a Part of God's Global Action
By Paul Borthwick
Gabriel Resources (1999), 250pp.
✫

Let the Nations Be Glad:
The Supremacy of God in Missions, Second Edition
By John Piper
Baker Book House (2003), 255 pp.
✫✫✫ (Puts God back in the center of missions.)

Let the Whole World Know:
Resources for Preaching on Missions
By Richard R. DeRidder and Roger S. Greenway
Baker (1998), 203 pp.
✩✩ (Sermon outlines, illustrations, and fresh insights into missions.)

Let's Quit Kidding Ourselves About Missions
By James M. Weber
Moody Press (1979), 138 pp.
✩

Living in Latin America — A Case Study
in Cross-Cultural Communication
By Raymond L. Gorden
National Textbook Co. (1985), 177 pp.
✩

Marching to a Different Drummer: Rediscovering Missions in
an Age of Affluence and Self-Interest
By Jim Raymo
Christian Literature Crusade (1996), 216 pp.
✩✩✩ (Possibly the best practical missions book printed in the last seven years. Deals with controversies well.)

A Mind for Missions: Ten Ways to Build Your World Vision
By Paul Borthwick
NavPress (1987), 167 pp.
✩

Ministering Cross-Culturally:
An Incarnational Model for Personal Relationships
By Sherwood G. Lingenfelter and Marvin K. Mayers
Baker (1986), 125 pp.
✩

The Mission of the Church in the World: A Biblical Theology
By Roger E. Hedlund
Baker (1991), 300 pp.
✩

Mission Handbook 2000-2003:
U.S. and Canadian Christian Ministries Overseas
(Mission Handbook, 18th Ed.)
By John A. Siewert and Dotsey Welliver, eds.
EMIS (2000), 504 pp.
✩✩ (Excellent resource on mission agencies.)

Mission Mobilizers Handbook
By Dave Imboden
William Carey Library (1996), 134 pp.
✩ (Key resources and articles for maximizing your church/
fellowship's impact.)

Mission Work in Today's World: Insights and Outlook
By J. Samuel Hofman
William Carey Library (1993), 210 pp.
✩

Missionary Methods: St. Paul's or Ours?
By Roland Allen
Eerdmans (1962), 179 pp.
✩✩✩

Missions USA
By Earl Parvin
Moody Press (1985), 381 pp.
✩

The New Context of World Mission
By Bryant L. Myers
Marc Publications (1996), 61 pp.
✩✩

On Being a Missionary
By Thomas Hale
William Carey Library (1995), 422 pp.
✩✩

Operation World: When We Pray God Works
By Patrick Johnstone and Jason Mandryk
Authentic Media (2000), 672 pp.
☆☆☆ (Maps, statistics, culture, missions, evangelism, and discipleship in every country.)

Out of the Comfort Zone
By George Verwer
Authentic Media (2000), 176 pp.
☆☆☆

Perspectives on the World Christian Movement:
A Reader (New & Revised Edition)
By Ralph D. Winter, Steven C. Hawthorne,
and Darrell R. Dorr, eds.
William Carey Library (1999), 782 pp.
☆☆☆ (Absolutely encyclopedic treatment of the mission movement.)

Planting Churches Cross-Culturally:
North America and Beyond
By David Hesselgrave and Donald Anderson McGavran
Baker (2nd ed. 2000), 462 pp.
☆

The Poor Have Faces:
Loving Your Neighbor in the 21st Century
By John Ronsvalle and Sylvia Ronsvalle
Baker (1992), 156 pp.
☆

Run With the Vision:
A Remarkable Global Plan for the 21st Century Church
By Bob Sjogren, Bill Stearns, and Amy Stearns
Bethany House (1995), 288 pp.
☆☆ (A good source on how to mobilize, how to send, and how to go.)

Scripture and Strategy:
The Use of the Bible in Postmodern Church and Mission
By David J. Hesselgrave
William Carey Library (1994), 192 pp.
☆ (Looks at whether our methods and strategies are based on the Word of God.)

Serving as Senders: How to Care for Your Missionaries
While They Are Preparing to Go, While They Are on the
Field, When They Return Home
By Neal Pirolo
Emmaus Road Intl. (1991), 208 pp.
☆☆ (A very practical help for evangelical sending churches.)

Six Dangerous Questions
To Transform Your View of the World
By Paul Borthwick
InterVarsity Press (1997), 129 pp.
☆☆

Successful Mission Teams: A Guide for Volunteers
By Martha VanCise
New Hope (1998), 231 pp.
☆

A Vision for Missions
By Tom Wells
Banner of Truth (1985), 157 pp.
☆☆ (The missionary vision must begin with the leadership of God to "declare His glory among the nations.")

What in the World Is God Doing?
The Essentials of Global Missions
By C. Gordon Olson
Global Gospel Publishers (1998), 143 pp.
☆☆

Window on the World
By Daphne Spraggett with Jill Johnstone
Authentic Media (2000), 221 pp.
★★★ (Excellent for children, young people, and family prayer time.)

World Mission: An Analysis of the World Christian Movement — The Strategic Dimension
By Jonathan Lewis, Meg Crossman, and Stephen Hoke, eds.
William Carey Library (1994), 560 pp.
★

World Shapers:
A Treasury of Quotations from Great Missionaries
By Vinita Hampton and Carol Plueddemann, eds.
Harold Shaw (1991), 160 pp.
★★★

Your Mission, Should You Accept It:
An Introduction for World Christians
By Stephen Gaukroger
InterVarsity Press (1997), 144 pp.
★

HISTORY OF MISSIONS

A Concise History of the Christian World Mission
By J. Herbert Kane
Baker (1980), 216 pp.
★★

Evangelical Dictionary of World Missions
By A. Scott Moreau, Harold A. Netland,
Charles Edward, Van Engen, and David Burnett eds.
Baker (2000), 1168 pp.
★★

A History of Christianity in Africa
By Elizabeth Isichei
Eerdmans (1995), 432 pp.
☆☆

A History of Christian Missions
(Pelican History of the Church, Volume 6)
By Stephen Neill
Viking Press (1994), 528 pp.
☆

On Their Way Rejoicing
(The History and Role of the Bible in Africa)
By Ype Schaff
Paternoster, (1997), 254 pp.
☆

The Story of Faith Missions
By Klaus Fiedler
Chariot Victor (1994), 428 pp.
☆

LEADERSHIP IN MISSIONS

30 Days to Confident Leadership
By Bobb Biehl
Broadman & Holman (1998), 240 pp.
☆

Dynamic Spiritual Leadership: Leading Like Paul
By J. Oswald Sanders
Discovery Enterprises (1990), 224 pp.
☆☆☆

Future Leader
By Viv Thomas
Authentic Media (2002), pp. 202
☆

Leadership Handbook of Management and Administration
By James D. Berkley, ed.
Baker (1997), 524 pp.
☆

Spiritual Leadership:
Principles of Excellence for Every Believer
By J. Oswald Sanders
Moody Press (1994), 189 pp.
☆☆☆

MINISTRY TO NEEDY CHILDREN

Children in Crisis: A New Commitment
By Phyllis Kilbourn, ed.
Marc Publications (1996), 272 pp.
☆☆☆

Healing the Children of War: A Handbook for Ministry to
Children Who Have Suffered Deep Traumas
By Phyllis Kilbourn, ed.
Marc Publications (1995), 318 pp.
☆☆☆

Kids for the World:
A Guidebook for Children's Mission Resources
By Gerry Dueck
William Carey Library (1990), 159 pp.
☆

Reaching Children in Need:
What's Being Done—What You Can Do
By Patrick McDonald with Emma Garrow
Kingsway Publications, 190 pp.
☆☆

Sexually Exploited Children: Working to Protect and Heal
By Phyllis Kilbourn and Marjorie McDermid, eds.
Marc Publications, 324 pp.
☆☆☆

*Street Children: The Tragedy and Challenge of the World's
Millions of Modern-Day Oliver Twists*
By Andy Butcher
Gabriel Publishing (2003), 201 pp.
☆ ☆ ☆

Street Children: A Guide to Effective Ministry
By Phyllis Kilbourn, ed.
Marc Publications (1997), 253 pp.
☆ ☆ ☆

PREPARATION, SUPPORT RAISING & FURLOUGHS

Culture Shock: Dealing with Stress in Cross-Cultural Living
By Myron Loss
Encouragement Ministry (1983), 142 pp.
☆

*Friend Raising:
Building a Missionary Support Team That Lasts*
By Betty Barnett
Crown Ministries Intl. (1996), 180 pp.
☆

Getting Sent: A Relational Approach to Support Raising
By Pete Sommer
InterVarsity Press (1999), 204 pp.
☆ ☆ ☆

Living Overseas: A Book of Preparations
By Ted Ward
Macmillan (1984), 358 pp.
☆

Manual for Missionaries on Furlough
By Marjorie A. Collins
Out of print, last published by William Carey Library (1978)
☆

Missionary Care: Counting the Cost for World Evangelization
By Kelly O'Donnell, John Powell, Brent Lindquist, and
Kenneth Harder
William Carey Library (1991), 360 pp.
☆ (How to support your missionary.)

People Raising: A Practical Guide to Raising Support
By William P. Dillon
Moody Press (1993), 255 pp.
☆☆

Raising Resilient MKs
By Joy M. Bowers, ed.
Mission Training International, 510 pp.
☆

*Re-Entry: Making the Transition from Missions to Life at
Home*
By Peter Jordan
Crown Ministries Intl. (1996), 150 pp.
☆

Send Me! Your Journey to the Nations
By Steve Hoke and Bill Taylor
William Carey Library, 136 pp.
☆☆

Survival of the Fittest:
Keeping Yourself Healthy in Travel and Service Overseas
By Dr. Christine Aroney-Sine
Missions Advanced Research (1994), 109 pp.
☆ (A good handbook for healthy travel and ministry.)

Too Valuable to Lose:
Exploring the Causes and Cures of Missionary Attrition
By William D. Taylor, ed.
William Carey Library (1997), 308 pp.
☆☆ (Excellent resource.)

SPECIALIZED

Answering Islam: The Crescent in Light of the Cross
By Norman Geisler and Abdul Saleeb
Baker (2nd ed. 2002), 336 pp.
☆

Communicating Christ in Animistic Contexts
By Gailyn Van Rheenen
William Carey Library (1996 ed.), 342 pp.
☆

Evangelization and Church Growth:
Issues from the Asian Context
By Roger Hedlund
William Carey Library, 344 pp.
☆

Planting Churches in Muslim Cities: A Team Approach
By Greg Livingstone
Baker (1993), 272 pp.
☆

Serving With the Poor in Africa:Cases in Holistic Ministry
By Tetsunao Yamamori, Bryant L. Myers, Kwame Bediako,
and Larry Reed, eds.
Missions Advanced Research (1996), 230 pp.
☆

THEOLOGICAL ISSUES IN MISSIONS

A Biblical Theology of Missions
By George W. Peters
Moody Press (1972), 368 pp.
☆

Contextualization:Meanings, Methods, and Models
By David J. Hesselgrave and Edward Rommen
William Carey Library (2000), 281 pp.
☆ ☆

Missions in the Third Millennium:
21 Key Trends for the 21ˢᵗ Century
By Stan Guthrie
Authentic Media (2002), 225 pp.
☆ ☆ ☆

Mission on the Way: Issues in Mission Theology
By Charles Van Engen
Baker (1997), 306 pp.
☆

URBAN MISSIONS

Cities: Missions' New Frontier
By Roger S. Greenway and Timothy M. Monsma
Baker (2000 2ⁿᵈ ed.), 228 pp.
☆ ☆ ☆

Cry of the Urban Poor: Reaching the Slums of Today's
Megacities
By Viv Grigg
Marc Publications (1992), 295 pp.
☆

Discipling the City: A Comprehensive Approach to Urban
Missions
By Roger S. Greenway, ed.
Baker (1992 2ⁿᵈ ed.), 302 pp.
☆ ☆

Planting and Growing Urban Churches:
From Dream to Reality
By Harvie M. Conn, ed.
Baker (1997), 272 pp.
☆

Research in Church and Mission
By Viggo Sogaard
William Carey Library (1996), 284 pp.
☆

Endnotes

[1] Wendy Murray Zoba, "Youth Has Special Powers," *Christianity Today* 45, no.2 (2001): 56–61.

[2] Scott Thompkins and Sandi Thompkins, "The Short-Term Explosion," *Moody Monthly*, no. 101 (2000): 13–17.

[3] D. Wang, "Now, Who Is Not Ministering to China?" *Asian Report,* September/October 1999, p.1, in *Missions in the Third Millennium—21 Key Trends for the 21st Century,* by Stan Guthrie (Carlisle, UK: Paternoster, 2001), p. 85.

[4] Jim Lo in *Missions in the Third Millennium—21 Key Trends for the 21st Century,* by Stan Guthrie (Carlisle, UK: Paternoster, 2001), p. 88.

[5] Tom Steller, interview 11 November 1999, in *Missions in the Third_Millennium—21 Key Trends for the 21st Century,* by Stan Guthrie (Carlisle, UK: Paternoster, 2001), p. 89.

[6] Stan Guthrie, *Missions in the Third Millennium—21 Key Trends for the 21st Century,* (Carlisle, UK: Paternoster, 2001) p. 89.

[7] Andy Crouch, "A Testimony in Reverse," *Christianity Today* 45, no. 2 (2001) p. 71.

[8] Donald Rumsfeld, "Rumsfeld's Rules" <www.library.villanova.edu/vbl/bweb/rumsfeldsrules.pdf>.

[9] "Re-entry Challenges," University of Wisconsin, <www.wisc.edu/studyabroad>.

[10] Edward T. Ryan and Kevin C. Kain, "Primary Care: Health Advice and Immunizations for Travelers," 342 *New England Journal of Medicine* (2000): 1716–25.

[11] Robert Steffen, Martin Rickenbach, Urs Wilhelm, Andrée Helminger, and Meinrad Schär, "Health Problems after Travel to Developing Countries," 156 *Journal of Infectious Diseases* (1987): 84–91.

[12] Robert Steffen and Elaine C. Jong, "Travelers' and Immigrants' Health," in *Tropical Infectious Diseases: Principles, Pathogens, and Practices,* by Richard L. Guerrant, David H. Walker and Peter F. Weller, eds. (Philadelphia: Churchill Livingstone, 1999), pp. 106–14.

[13] Steffen, Rickenbach, Wilhelm, Helminger, and Schär, *Journal of Infectious Diseases* 156 (1987): 84–91.

[14] Daniel Reid and Jay S. Keystone, "Health Risks Abroad: General Considerations," in *Textbook of Travel Medicine and Health*, by Herbert L. DuPont and Robert Steffen, eds. (Hamilton, Ont.: B.C. Decker, 1997), 3–9.

[15] Reid and Keystone, in *Textbook of Travel Medicine and Health* (Hamilton, Ont.: B.C. Decker, 1997), 3–9.

[16] S.W. Hargarten, T.D. Baker, and K. Guptill, "Overseas Fatalities of United States Citizen Travelers: An Analysis of Deaths Related to International Travel," *Annals of Emergency Medicine* 20 (1991): 622–26.

[17] Adapted from <www.travelhealth.com/purwtr.htm>.

[18] Adapted from S. Blythe, Travel Health Information Service <www.travelhealth.com>.

[19] Ryan and Kain, 342 *New England Journal of Medicine* (2000): 1716–25.

[20] V. De Leo, "Contact Dermatitis: Photocontact Dermatitis." *Immunology and Allergy Clinics of North America* no. 17 (1997): 451–469 (Table 3).

[21] Patrick M. Malone and Margot Melville, "Drug-Induced Photosensitivity," *Micromedex* 115 (2003).

[22] Ryan and Kain, 342 *New England Journal of Medicine* (2000): 1716–25.

[23] Ryan and Kain, 342 *New England Journal of Medicine* (2000): 1716–25.

[24] Travel to Developing Countries <www.mdconsult.com/das/patient/body/0/41/5447.html>.

[25] Ryan and Kain, 342 *New England Journal of Medicine* (2000): 1716–25.

[26] Sources for this appendix include "Recommended Adult Immunization Schedule United States, 2002–2003 and Recommended Immunizations for Adults with Medical Conditions

(January 18, 2003) <www.cdc.gov/nip/recs/adult-schedule-508.htm> and "Update on Adult Immunization Recommendations of the Immunization Practices Advisory Committee" (May 5, 2002) <www.cdc.gov/mmwr/preview/mmwrhtml/00025228.htm>. I also consulted Ryan and Kain, 342 *New England Journal of Medicine* (2000): 1716–25.

[27] United Nations Disaster Response Organization, in "Disaster Response: When Good Intentions Aren't Enough," Interaction, American Council for Voluntary International Action <www.vita.org>.

[28] Adapted from Virtual Disaster Library, Pan American Health Organization (1999) <www.paho.org>.

[29] United Nations Disaster Response Organization, in "Disaster Response: When Good Intentions Aren't Enough," Interaction, American Council for Voluntary International Action <www.vita.org>.

[30] Andrew Natsios, in "Disaster Response: When Good Intentions Aren't Enough," Interaction, American Council for Voluntary International Action <www.vita.org>.

[31] "*A World Safe from Natural Disasters—The Journey of Latin America and the Caribbean,*" (Pan American Health Organization) p. 57, <www. paho.org/English/PED/ws-chapter5.pdf>.

[32] Modified from a list compiled by Doug Nichols, international director of Action International Ministries, and originally published at <www.epm.org/missbooks.html>. Used with permission.

Other books available from...

Gabriel
Publishing

PO Box 1047
129 Mobilization Dr
Waynesboro, GA 30830

706-554-1594
1-8MORE-BOOKS
gabriel@omlit.om.org

Cat and Dog Theology
Rethinking Our Relationship With Our Master

Bob Sjogren & Dr. Gerald Robison

There is a joke about cats and dogs that conveys their differences perfectly.

> A dog says, "You pet me, you feed me, you shelter me, you love me, you must be God."
> A cat says, "You pet me, you feed me, you shelter me, you love me, I must be God."

These God-given traits of cats ("You exist to serve me") and dogs ("I exist to serve you") are often similar to the theological attitudes we have in our view of God and our relationship to Him. Using the differences between cats and dogs in a light-handed manner, the authors compel us to challenge our thinking in deep and profound ways. As you are drawn toward God and the desire to reflect His glory in your life, you will worship, view missions, and pray in a whole new way. This life-changing book will give you a new perspective and vision for God as you delight in the God who delights in you.

1884543170   206 Pages

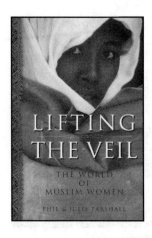

Lifting the Veil
The World of Muslim Women

Phil and Julie Parshall

Secluded from the eyes of anyone but family members, Muslim women live under a system of tradition, rites and rituals that favor men above women. "A man loves first his son, then his camel, and then his wife," says an Arab proverb.

Phil and Julie Parshall understand the issues, heartaches and dangers facing Muslim women today, having lived among them for more than four decades. They bring a sensitive perspective to this thoughtful, yet sobering book that examines the controversy of female circumcision and proof of virginity, the heartache of arranged marriages, divorce, polygamy, and the status of women living in a male dominated world.

This book will not provide you with easy answers but will prompt you to begin praying for these "daughters of Ishmael," and give you sensitive awareness to life behind the veil.

1884543677   288 Pages

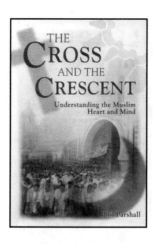

The Cross and The Crescent
Understanding the Muslim Heart and Mind

Phil Parshall

Who are the Muslims?

You hear about them in the news every day. Many people associate them with terrorism and cruelty. Some admire their willingness to die for their faith. Others wonder if there is more to Islam than fanaticism and martyrdom. And Christians ask, "How do we respond in faith and love to these people?" This question is more pressing than ever.

Phil Parshall understands the Muslim heart and mind. Living as a missionary among Muslims, he knows them - not as a band of fanatics on the evening news, but as individuals, some good, some bad. In this very warm, very personal book he looks at what Muslims believe and how their beliefs affect and often don't affect their behavior. He compares and contrasts Muslim and Christian views on the nature of God, sacred Scriptures, worship, sin and holiness, mysticism, Jesus and Muhammed, human suffering and the afterlife.

1884543685   320 Pages

Leading the Way
Leadership is Not Just for Super Christians

Paul Borthwick

As we enter a new millennium, there is a growing vacuum of leadership among the younger generation. The need is great for younger men and women who will rise to the challenge - in the face of great opportunities and great obstacles - to be obedient to the call of leadership.

This is the rallying call Paul Borthwick puts forth in *Leading The Way*. He asserts that leadership is not just reserved for those with the "right" education, abilities, status or background. Rather, God is calling all young Christians who have the vision and responsibility to persevere, to fill this growing leadership vacuum.

There are so many areas of need in the world, and so few young people who seem willing to lead the way in meeting those needs. That means there are leadership positions enough for anyone with the commitment and interest necessary to heed the call!

1884543871   248 Pages

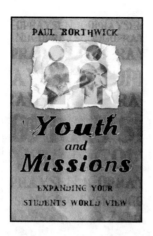

Youth and Missions
Expanding your Students' World View

Paul Borthwick

Take a group of teenagers – of all shapes, sizes, and spiritual maturity. Add the challenge of sharing Jesus Christ in both familiar and unfamiliar cultures. Mix in ample amounts of preparation, good role models, cross cultural exposure and experience, adventure and affirmation. Season with Bible study and prayer. It all adds up to a dynamic recipe for spiritual growth that can turn your youth group members into world Christians.

Youth and Missions is a practical handbook filled with principles, guidelines, and examples of how to help young people to grow in their understanding of the world and their part in it. It provides a basic step-by-step approach to:

- motivating youth toward world missions
- modeling world concern
- exposing group members to missions opportunities in the church, youth group, and at home
- providing "life changing" missions experiences
- promoting "long-term" results in students' lives

188454388X   256 Pages

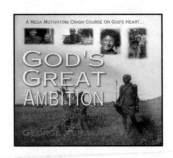

God's Great Ambition
A Mega-Motivating Crash Course on God's Heart

Dan and Dave Davidson
and George Verwer

This unique collection of quotes and Scriptures has been designed to motivate thousands of people into action in world missions. George Verwer and the Davidsons are well-known for their ministries of mission mobilization as speakers and writers.

Turn to any page and get ready to be encouraged and respond with an increase of awareness, action and ownership in sharing God's good news around His world.

1884543693   208 Pages

Operation World
Patrick Johnstone & Jason Mandryk

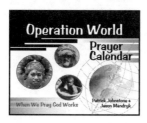

Prayer Calendar

This spiral desk calendar contains clear graphics and useful geographic, cultural, economic, and political statistics on 122 countries of the world. The *Operation World Prayer Calendar* is a great tool to help you pray intelligently for the world. Pray for each country for three days and see how God works!

1884543596   256 Pages

Wall Map
22" x 36"

This beautiful, full-color wall map is a great way to locate the countries that you are praying for each day and build a global picture. Not only an excellent resource for schools, churches, and offices, but a valuable tool for the home.

188454360X   Laminated
1884543618   Folded